# FOOTWEAR DESIGN

**LAURENCE KING**

Copyright © text Aki Choklat 2012

Published in 2012 by
Laurence King Publishing Ltd
361–373 City Road, London,
EC1V 1LR, United Kingdom
T +44 20 7841 6900
F +44 20 7841 6910
enquiries@laurenceking.com
www.laurenceking.com

Reprinted 2013

A catalogue record for this book is available
from the British Library.

ISBN: 978 1 85669 745 3

Design by Melanie Mues,
Mues Design, London

Senior Editor Melissa Danny

Printed in China

**Front cover**
**Top** Julia Lundsten/FINSK/www.finsk.com
Photo James Frid
**Center** Aku Bäckström
**Bottom** Cherry-red "Madlene" ankle boot
in suede/photo Esther Teichmann/courtesy
Max Kibardin

**Back cover**
**Top** Laura Schannach
**Bottom** Jin Hong

# FOOTWEAR DESIGN

**AKI CHOKLAT**

**LAURENCE KING PUBLISHING**

# CONTENTS

Related study material is available on the Laurence King website at www.laurenceking.com

*A shoe can transform you and make you feel like a different person. This shoe by Heather Blake is harmonious, elegant, and, above all, sexy.*

# INTRODUCTION

This book is the response to a simple need: there was no shoe-design manual in existence. *Footwear Design* will help you to understand the processes involved in shoe design, and to develop and design a comprehensive footwear collection based on your personally researched material. It will also answer some of the questions that you might have about the industry.

The book is divided into six chapters, starting with the history of footwear. This chapter not only takes a chronological approach but also explores how we learn from the past and make connections with the present. In the second chapter we will familiarize ourselves with the anatomy of the foot and the basic components of a shoe, building up an understanding of how the foot and the shoe work together.

However, the essential emphasis of *Footwear Design* is in chapters three and four: Research and Collection Design respectively. In the Research section we explain how to take inspiration and translate it into a dynamic collection of shoes; in Collection Design we explore some of the numerous creative exercises that can help you with your design development, including draping and silhouette exercises.

Chapter five covers basic illustration styles, and effective ways to present your work (including portfolios). By this point you will be able to produce a full factory-ready design package that includes the starting point (mood), the illustrations (creative view), and technical specifications (materials, color, and flats).

Finally, chapter six discusses career and educational opportunities and offers preliminary information for those who want to explore further options. We have sourced work from museum archives, designer archives, and collections the world over, and we have interviewed successful designers, academics, makers, and trend forecasters in order to demonstrate the variety of the industry.

*Footwear Design* has been written in order to encourage personal experience, individuality, and independent thinking in design. It is about bringing new creativity to the world of shoes.

# CHAPTER 1
# FOOTWEAR DESIGN
# THEN AND NOW

**Footwear design is perhaps one of the oldest occupations known to man. Footwear has always had one basic function—to protect feet from the elements—yet even the first, simple forms of foot protection showed a glimpse of early shoe design. This chapter does not pretend to be a comprehensive timeline, but rather shows a selection of historical inspirations.**

Human beings' love affair with shoes may go back to prehistoric times, although no actual piece of footwear from that time exists. The first, indirect evidence of primitive footwear dates back 40,000 years, when the bone structure of the little toe started to change—an indication that humans were wearing something on their feet. Some of the earliest preserved shoes date from 9,500 years ago, and were discovered in 1938 in central Oregon by Luther Cressman of the University of Oregon. These were a type of closed-toe flat shoe made from twined rope and look surprisingly modern. The oldest preserved leather shoe is a recent discovery from a cave in Armenia, which dates back to about 5,000 years ago. This molded moccasin-type shoe was held together with a strap of leather and filled with hay for comfort and insulation, showing that already many aspects of contemporary footwear design had been taken into consideration: fit, look, and comfort.

Visual references to footwear appear throughout history, from 5,000-year-old Spanish cave paintings to the ancient Egyptian, Greek, and Oriental art now seen in all the major museums of the world. Many interesting sandal and shoe styles are depicted in these artworks, reinforcing the sense that fashion footwear has a very long and rich history. Not only have shoes evolved in tandem with one of the most important of human activities—walking—but they often give us clues as to the social status of the wearer, and much more besides.

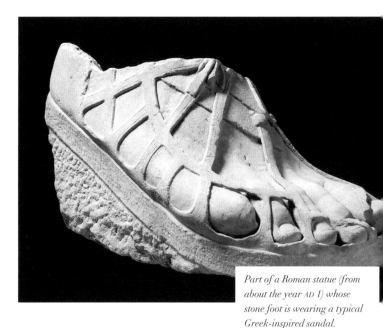

*Part of a Roman statue (from about the year AD 1) whose stone foot is wearing a typical Greek-inspired sandal. Some museum pieces offer fascinating insights into the history of footwear.*

*These flat shoes, made from twine rope, date back 10,000 years, demonstrating the long heritage of material and design innovation.*

*These Armenian shoes are extremely well preserved, showing how leather was already being used for footwear over 5,000 years ago.*

But how does this evidence of early footwear serve the modern-day designer? A study of the history of footwear is not only rewarding, but essential. It is important to understand how the history of footwear has evolved, from the construction of shoes to their cultural significance: the knowledge of your craft's past can make you a better designer. Most modern footwear components exist because of developments in the past, deriving both from experience of wear and from research. Early footwear styles can also offer some surprising solutions and inspiration on many levels, such as for closures and ornamentation.

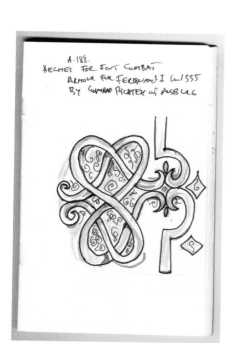

*Eighteenth-century postillion boots (known as gambadoe) that were designed to protect the wearer's feet while on horseback—historic footwear with a modern silhouette.*

*These 1790s low-heeled pointy shoes are fitted with an overshoe, made to protect the wearer's shoes and feet from the dirty streets of the time.*

*Museums offer great inspiration but most do not allow photography, so keep a notebook and writing instrument handy at all times. The ornamentation in this shoe was inspired by a carving in a 1555 metal helmet (left).*

The footwear of the past often displayed the same extravagance as that of many modern designs. One only needs to look at sixteenth-century chopines to understand that women have always had a desire to stand tall and confident. Chopines were platform shoes that were popular with Venetian courtesans. They originated from the idea of an overshoe, or elevated shoe, that helped to avoid the dirt when walking in the soiled streets of the time. The extreme height (sometimes as high as 20 in.) soon proved not to be very practical, as the wearers often needed help just to walk in them. Recent trends are echoing chopines, as heels and platforms once again reach dizzying heights.

Another extreme fashion statement from the Renaissance period were poulaines, which were popular with men. These were shoes whose pointed toes became longer and longer as the fashion went to extremes. The length grew to a stage where it would actually prevent the wearer from being able to walk—unless the ends were tied around his ankles. Sometimes the long points were supported by whale bones. As with many trends in the history of dress, the length of one's poulaines differed according to the wearer's social standing. Basic survival needs soon put an end to this fashion: long poulaines hindered a swift escape from one's enemies. The lesson to be learned here is that there was no real reason for the shoes to be so long, except to follow fashion.

*These sixteenth-century Venetian chopines prove that extreme footwear is not a new concept.*

*Noritaka Tatehana's shoes usually come in dizzying heights; they are a contemporary chopine of sorts.*

*The long points of poulaines had no practical purpose, just a fashionable one.*

*In modern times identities can be expressed through footwear, as seen in this picture of the band Leningrad Cowboys.*

# FASHION AND CELEBRITY —THE SEVENTEENTH AND EIGHTEENTH CENTURIES

The seventeenth and eighteenth centuries in Western Europe saw increased trade with distant lands. New surface design elements, such as embroidery and appliqué, were introduced to the footwear market. Exquisitely expensive materials and accessories were used on shoes to match the extravagance of the clothes of the period. Only the upper echelons could afford these intricately decorated shoes, which were generally made from textiles for men and women alike. Some commoners' versions—cheaper imitations of the fancier shoes—were, however, also available. They can be seen today in museum archives, and prove the point that celebrity-driven fashions have been around longer than one might expect. In contrast, leather shoes were generally more utilitarian and worn by the lower classes.

Another "trend" that evolved during this time in Europe—one that was introduced at the court of Louis XIV—was the wearing of the red heel, or *talon rouge*. Initially an aristocratic status symbol, the red heel soon became an item of footwear that was also adopted in other parts of European society.

Men and women started to abandon high heels at the time of the French Revolution with the end of the aristocracy's dominance, and heel height became more sensible. High heels for women would not make a comeback until the middle of the nineteenth century, while men did not start wearing heels again until the 1970s.

*Red heels were once all the rage in European courts; they are seen here on Louis XIV in this portrait from 1701.*

*Queen Henrietta Maria's shoes from the seventeenth century were the ultimate luxury items of their time— made of silk and crimson velvet, with raised sequins and silver thread embroidery.*

# HAUTE COUTURE AND SEASONAL FASHION CYCLES—THE NINETEENTH CENTURY

In the second half of the nineteenth century, as wealth began to expand among the upper-middle classes, life in high society sparked notions of grandeur. Haute couture was born, and fashion started to follow the cyclical pattern of seasons. The improvement in walking conditions and the introduction of paved streets in the bigger cities allowed women to walk in higher heels again. The looks for fashion footwear were heavily influenced by Paris—at that time the cultural capital of the world. This was the period when the contemporary footwear silhouette as we know it today started to take shape, together with the early beginnings of sports-related footwear.

# INNOVATION AND STREET FASHION—THE TWENTIETH CENTURY

The beginning of the twentieth century heralded two developments in the footwear industry: the introduction of industrialization and the adoption by the youth of America of rubber-soled shoes—originally intended for sportswear—as everyday fashion.

The footwear industry in Europe was, however, held back for many years as a result of the two World Wars, when many tanneries and shoe factories were employed in the war effort. Innovative footwear for women was instead made from nonrationed materials such as straw and wood.

The 1930s and 1940s witnessed the genius of Salvatore Ferragamo, Italian icon of footwear design. Ferragamo was a true innovator, who patented many of his ideas. His highly original wedges were shortly followed by the modern conception of platform shoes. The metal shank, an integral part of today's footwear construction, was another one of his innovations. Ferragamo was also one of the first footwear designers to be inspired by the world around him—including archaeological discoveries, architecture, and the modern art of the age—which has become fundamental to the contemporary concept of footwear design.

In the 1950s another invention was born—the stiletto. Ferragamo and Roger Vivier of France pioneered a shoe with a high, narrow, pinlike heel, which made headlines in this postwar era. Previously heels were made either from wood or stacked leather, but the postwar development in steelmaking techniques allowed these new types of tall, thin heels to be widely produced using industrial processes—demonstrating the value of cross-pollinating ideas between industries (something that is encouraged in today's design environment as well, see p. 83). The world is full of

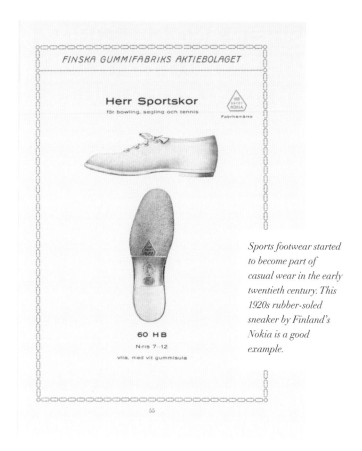

*Sports footwear started to become part of casual wear in the early twentieth century. This 1920s rubber-soled sneaker by Finland's Nokia is a good example.*

innovations and ideas that are just waiting to find their place in different industries, including footwear. New areas of research, such as nanotechnology, are bringing us ideas that previously sounded wildly futuristic. The innovations are there: it simply takes designers to find a place for them in the creation of footwear, just as Ferragamo did in his day. Drawing on knowledge of the history of footwear design, today's designer should not be afraid to experiment with unusual materials and ideas.

The second half of the century saw the rise of street style as a source of inspiration in fashion design. London store Biba opened its doors in 1964, offering fashion items seen on TV and music idols at an affordable price. A popular shoe style of the 1960s was a low-heeled boot, also called the go-go boot, which was made into a commercial fashion item by André Courrèges and then widely copied by other fashion houses.

*The Salvatore Ferragamo wedge (1942) was a sensational invention that spread the world over, and continues to be one of the most popular styles today.*

The early 1970s saw many creations that took shoes to new heights—literally. British glam rock, which developed in post-hippy Britain, influenced the young street style of the day, and this signaled the return of heels for men. A few years later it was the turn of another youth movement to completely change everything in fashion. In 1976–77 punk exploded onto the fashion scene and although not everyone subscribed to its more flamboyant extremes, its influence permeated the fashion world. The punk footwear of choice was militant and authentic, a look perfectly expressed by Dr. Martens boots. Current footwear still shows traces of this legacy, and studs and military boots are still very much associated with the punk look.

Fashion in the 1980s began by taking references from street culture. New Romantic ideas started to filter through, and one of the most iconic leg silhouettes of the 1980s involved the pixie boot—a slightly pointed ankle boot with either a folded or a creased leg, worn by both men and women. This decade also saw sneaker culture take shape. The 1980s aerobic fad inspired new fashionable sneaker styles, with Reebok's Freestyle to the fore. The women's version of the shoe initially was designed for the gym but crossed over to streetwear, and sportswear and streetwear started to merge. The end of the 1980s marked the beginning of an economic decline, which was reflected in dress styles. Dressing down became acceptable, and this fed the casual sneaker culture.

In the 1990s a contemporary idea of luxury started to form. Fashion houses realized that the consumer could easily buy into the designer dream via accessories such as shoes. Prada's red-striped heel sport shoe, for example, became one of the best branded products of the decade. Prada also initiated the idea of a hybrid shoe, mixing sport construction with luxurious upper materials; this would be echoed in the Prada nylon aesthetic of mixing luxury and performance. Sneaker companies also started to push ideas further and further, creating a new sneaker culture that has not shown any sign of slowing down.

*Punk rock left a long-lasting impression on the way youth dressed; military-inspired boots such as Dr. Martens were the shoes of choice for punks.*

*Men's high heels were virtually nonexistent for nearly 200 years, until their return during the 1970s glam scene; they are worn here by David Bowie.*

# THE FUTURE OF FOOTWEAR DESIGN—THE TWENTY-FIRST CENTURY

In the twenty-first century *Sex and the City* became one of the most successful television series in the world. Sarah Jessica Parker (pretty much single-handedly) changed women's attitudes toward spending money on shoes, making footwear the most important luxury item to be had. The show also made Manolo Blahnik, Jimmy Choo, and Christian Louboutin household names the world over. Nowadays designers such as Stuart Weitzman (featured here) aren't just for the red carpet—glamorous shoes are increasingly featured in daily wear. It could be said that history is repeating itself, and the extravagance of footwear is back.

*Stuart Weitzman's feather-decorated shoes echo the spirit of the* Sex and the City *generation.*

*This diamond-studded shoe by Stuart Weitzman became the ultimate red-carpet accessory, with a value of $2 million.*

*In the new millennium the* Sex and the City *TV series pushed footwear to the top of the must-have fashion item list.*

What is the future of footwear design? It is exciting that each year several hundred new footwear design graduates start their careers. Some may start their own labels, while others join companies to work as in-house designers. The current footwear design community has many innovative thinkers who push design concepts ever further. Marloes ten Bhömer, for example, has reinvented the concept of the metal shank, and constantly develops innovative ideas in construction. Julia Lundsten of FINSK is re-creating the shoe silhouette in her less commercial projects. Conceptual designers such as Bart Hess and fashion designers such as Rick Owens keep pushing the silhouette in order to bring new ideas to an otherwise oversaturated world of shoe design. The future of shoe design looks very promising indeed.

*Julia Lundsten's FINSK shoe creates a visually interesting modern product by incorporating height and marrying the upper with an architectural platform bottom.*

*Bart Hess keeps pushing the boundaries of design, creating material-driven concepts such as these hairy "living" shoes.*

*Marloes ten Bhömer's innovative footwear is made from a single piece of leather and a reinvented metal shank/heel combination.*

*Rick Owens always manages to offer something different with his creations; note especially the silhouette of the foot and volume of the material.*

# THE FOOTWEAR INDUSTRY

Footwear continues to enjoy the spotlight in the fashion world. Shoe designers have become internationally famous, while magazines and fashion supplements feature footwear as one of the most critical fashion accessories.

There is a definite focus on footwear in high-street (mass-market chain) stores. The most sought-after "it" items from the catwalks are no longer always bags but often shoes. The New York flagship store of the high-end US retail chain Saks Fifth Avenue boasts a footwear department so big that it has its own postal code. London's Selfridges store has the world's largest footwear department, housing more than 55,000 pairs of shoes and catering to the true shoe obsessive: during its launch in 2010, store-wide marketing—from window-dressing to visual merchandising—was dedicated to all things footwear-related. Fast-fashion companies, understanding the importance of footwear, have brought about an increase in the presence of shoes, even within clothing stores.

Footwear has also become more popular in online retail. American-based Zappos.com was one of the first online retailers to break through consumers' resistance to buying shoes online by offering excellent customer service, which included a postage-free returns service. Zappos has led the online footwear boom, achieving sales worth more than $1 billion in 2008. They have basically done the same thing that Amazon did for bookselling. In fact in 2010 Zappos decided to join Amazon to continue with the same level of customer service and push further with e-commerce activities. Amazon also has its separate growing footwear department under the name of Javari. Other retail giants, such as Gap (with its Piperlime footwear division) and Topshop (who continue to push their online presence), follow suit. Footwear offers a lucrative platform for many companies to sell a trend-driven product that fits pretty much every body type.

The media have also fully embraced the sexy world of shoes. Footwear features heavily on fashion websites, blogs, and portals. Such magazines as *Elle* and *Vogue* are full of the latest must-have shoes, and offer seasonal accessories guides for fashion-hungry consumers. The media focus on footwear is very much a new phenomenon. Fashion magazines from before the 1990s show a concentration on clothing; shoes and shoe brands were hardly mentioned in, much less the main focus of, features or fashion photography. In the 1990s luxury fashion houses realized that shoes offered another gateway to luxury. During the same period, production slowly began to move away from Europe to the Far East, making complicated fashion footwear more affordable to the average consumer.

*Selfridges celebrates the opening of its new footwear department by making footwear-related displays across all departments in this flagship London store.*

# INNOVATION

Today the footwear industry is one of the most exciting fashion markets in the world, but also one of the most saturated. This is clear in mass-market fashion, where thousands of labels are showing an incredible number of styles, all screaming "Buy me!". Many fast-fashion brands have racks of trend-driven footwear that can be impulse-purchased along with the cheap sweaters and T-shirts. This type of retail lacks innovative thinking, but nevertheless plays an important part in modern fashion culture.

However, one area that does not lack innovation is performance footwear design. Thanks to the bigger product-development budgets of performance footwear companies, innovation is a top priority within their business. Many of the sneaker brands are performance-driven, and are constantly looking to push their concepts further. One example of footwear design that has incorporated new technology is the Nike+ sports kit. It involves Nike shoes with built-in transmitters that link to an iPod (or another enabled device), allowing the wearer to monitor his or her exercise regime.

Another performance-driven new concept is MBT (Masai Barefoot Technology)—"physiological footwear" that mimics the way we walk when barefoot, inspired by the Masai people of East Africa. The rocking motion these shoes encourage allegedly helps to tone the bottom and calf muscles. This idea has been adopted by many other sport labels and even young-fashion shoe labels. Nevertheless, fashion forward thinking is often lacking in performance footwear. This is most likely due to companies setting strict design guidelines to fit the numerous restrictions and corporate directives. These guidelines are an effort to protect the brand and company interests, rather than encouraging forward design thinking. Children's shoes have also seen some interesting developments in recent years—for example, Heelys (sneaker brand with built-in roller wheels) and shoes with step-activated lights. While these are obviously novelty products, they contain simple innovation that could spark new ideas in the rest of the footwear market as well.

But why is it that there is such a limited amount of innovative thinking in footwear? One possible reason is the great complexity of the manufacturing process; making a pair of shoes is time-consuming and requires great expertise. It is possible to create smaller production lines for clothes, but for shoes this is often not an option. Footwear production needs to be reinvented in such a way as to provide a more accessible platform for creating new styles and types of footwear.

One area of footwear design that requires a new way of thinking is the "eco" footwear market. Global demands on footwear companies' ethical stance has presented challenges in design and production. Some have explored making shoes without glue (only using stitching) while others have constructed shoes from recycled materials such as used car tires. The design challenge is often how to make ethical and sustainable footwear sexy. There are many areas that can be environmentally considered in shoe manufacturing, but it is very difficult to achieve a

*Sustainability is one of the areas in footwear design and production that is growing every year. These shoes by Oat are completely biodegradable.*

100 percent "green" shoe. However, there is continuous research on how to make a more sustainable shoe—a top priority for many footwear companies. This quest is no longer just about using environmentally friendly materials and construction methods, but also about other indirect processing factors such as the improvement of work conditions, and offsetting the carbon emissions caused by transportation. Many companies are looking into producing more efficiently and wasting less.

Companies such as Puma have completely rethought the way they do packaging, offering a new type of shoe box/bag that will produce 65 percent less waste than the old shoe boxes. While many larger companies are actively trying to consider more ecological options, many designers are interested in a sustainable approach as well, so there is a growing number of "green" brands emerging. A label called Oat is one of the first brands to offer a completely biodegradable product. And Stella McCartney has maintained ethical credibility by not using leather in her accessories collections, yet being able to provide highly desirable products. The future of footwear design lies in finding new ways to deal with the increasing global ecological and ethical demands.

## FUTURE TRENDS

There are designers who do continue to push design boundaries —Kei Kagami (below) and Eelko Moorer (opposite) being two good examples as they have both shown new ways of looking at how people walk and how to construct a shoe. Kei Kagami is not

limited to the shape of the foot, and has created volume outside the shoe by using simple ideas such as extended lasts, heels, and materials that are not often used in footwear, e.g., fiberglass. Moorer has a product developer approach to his footwear design, often analyzing the relationship of the components of the shoe and the foot.

But what does the future hold for footwear? Numerous fast-developing new technologies will certainly influence how we design, wear, and think about footwear. Nanotechnology in particular—science at a subatomic level—holds great promise for many industries. This technology has made extended water-repellency combined with breathability possible in the textile industry. Many other innovations in nanotechnology, such as increased flexibility and lightness, or the ability to create color by changing the very nature of materials, provide a new vision for footwear as well. High-tech ideas that may be applied to the footwear industry in the near future are constantly in development. The footwear design business is one of the biggest fashion industries in the world, yet it is affected by the same external factors as many other industries. Climate change, economics, and constantly changing trends provide both stimulation and challenges to the design community. However, as long as footwear designers continue to produce interesting and beautiful shoes, the shoe business will continue to thrive.

*Kei Kagami's use of material with this fiberglass and leather combination shoe solidifies liquid movement.*

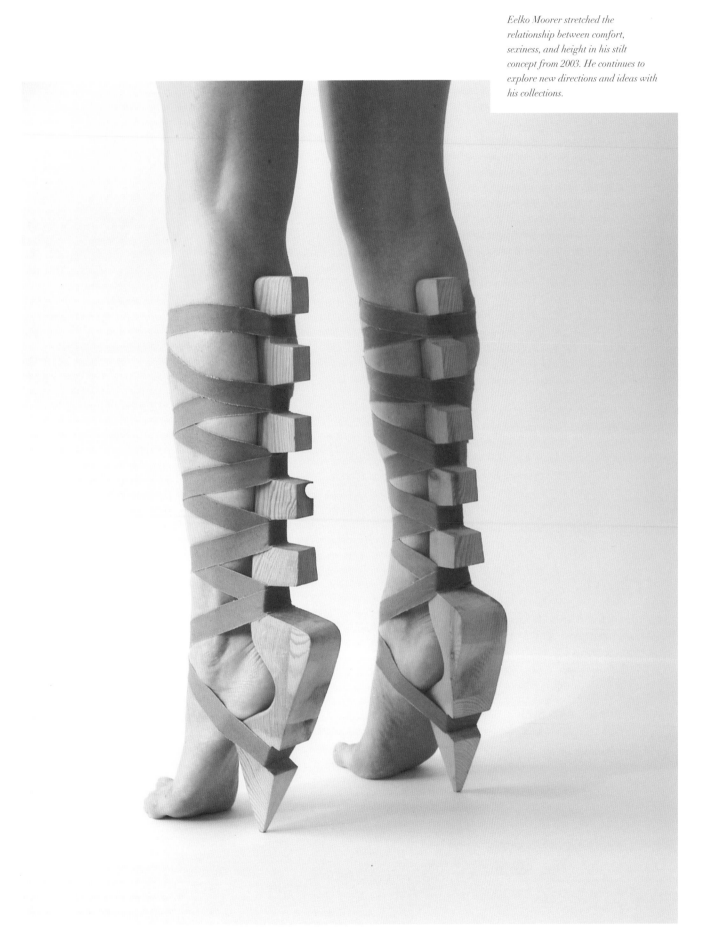

Eelko Moorer stretched the relationship between comfort, sexiness, and height in his stilt concept from 2003. He continues to explore new directions and ideas with his collections.

# CASE STUDY: LIZA SNOOK

Dutch footwear enthusiast and curator Liza Snook traces her love affair with shoes back to her early childhood, when she saw a pair of shoes in the window of an Italian store. Despite training as a graphic artist she has, since her childhood, been interested in all things relating to footwear. The Virtual Shoe Museum is an online gallery and portal that celebrates all things footwear. Its origins go back to the mid-1980s, when Snook started to collect and archive shoe-related information from newspapers and magazines, as well as real shoes. She also has an extensive collection of Barbie shoes. The website is designed by Liza's partner, Taco Zwaanswijk.

**Q What is the purpose of the museum?**

**A** It started as a project to collect and categorize the shoes I liked best. Today it has become a worldwide network for shoe designers and shoe lovers and a source for journalists, publishers, and young talent. The core of our virtual collection focuses on designs that question the very essence of the shoe. Is this a shoe? Is this wearable? Does it matter? Is it tickling your imagination? Designs that balance between these values and still present a shoe that can be worn, or looks as if it could be worn, are what I'm after—a twist, a sense of humor.

**Q How do you choose material for the museum?**

**A** I like collecting designs, works of art, inspiring images, and objects, and in particular anything about shoes. My hunting grounds are very diverse: the Internet, flea markets, bookstores, museums. Now many artists find us and present their prototypes or designs to be included in our collection. In the beginning I relied on my own archive and personal interest in the shoe designer community. Of course in time you meet so many designers and artists, and I'm glad they find their way to us when they're working on a new collection.

**Q You also gather drawings and pretty much anything relating to footwear. Do you have some kind of a system?**

**A** Having a system, method, or protocol will inevitably exclude things that won't fit. The things that won't fit are in fact the ones that interest me most. They exist on the edge, and that's what I find interesting. So no, there is no list with qualifications or criteria you have to meet to be selected. Any proposed design will be judged on originality, influence, and potential, no matter who the designer is. Of course there are people I follow, because they keep reinventing themselves and I really admire this. But new talent is always welcome, since my museum doesn't have any limits on presentation space.

**Q Why do you think it is important to preserve some of the ideas you have gathered?**

**A** Preservation is important for various reasons. Most shoe designers are focused on their next collection, as they should be. Sometimes their current and previous collections can get dismissed. The Virtual Shoe Museum aims to present relevant work from any era, so designers and shoe lovers can be inspired by designs from all ages. Another reason is that many designs that are presented today mimic designs we have seen before. But the fashion industry is so committed to what's next that historical awareness is sometimes lacking. With our rooms dedicated to different themes, materials, colors, and focus we try to create a context for the designs of tomorrow. The final reason for preservation is that the Virtual Shoe Museum aims to be a platform for young talent. Shoe designers and artists can have direct contact with the curator of the museum. Mail is replied to quickly, and when a design is innovative and inspiring it will find its way to our homepage.

**Q What are your plans for the future?**

**A** We are hoping to set up a store, so we can start to earn funds to support the growth of the nonprofit initiative. One of the things we like to do is to connect and inspire people, share information. A new way of doing this has been to become a "non-virtual" space. Some of the products were presented in real time at fairs such as GDS in Düsseldorf (Germany) and the Dongguan (China) shoe fair.

**Q Can you mention some of the designers you feature?**

**A** Our virtual shoe collection includes a big variety of shoes: shoes made by designers and artists but also shoes made by architects, illustrators, and photographers. I admire designers such as Marloes ten Bhömer, Kobi Levi, and Ted Noten as well as artists such as Barbara Zucchi, Iris Schieferstein, and Svenja Ritter.

**Q What do shoes signify for you?**

**A** To me shoes are wearable art objects. They can make or break your outfit. The kind of shoes you choose show who you are: they are a public announcement, a personal touch to an outfit. So, be aware of your shoes!

**Q What advice can you give a future shoe-design hopeful?**

**A** Push the (shoe) design limits! Inspire and awe people. Go crazy, think weird, out of the box, and broaden your perspective.

*Liza's Snook's Virtual Shoe Museum provides a platform and a portal to a world that celebrates the diversity in footwear design. The content can be searched based on numerous indicators and end use, color, and materials.*

# CASE STUDY: CATHERINE WILLEMS

For the past ten years Catherine Willems has divided her time between the roles of designer, professor, and researcher. She teaches footwear design, including patterns and making, at the Faculty of Fine Arts at the University College Ghent in Belgium and is a guest lecturer in the Department of Fine Arts at the Royal Academy in The Hague, the Netherlands. She has also worked with internationally renowned fashion designers, including Walter Van Beirendonck, Haider Ackerman, and Tim Van Steenbergen, developing footwear for fashion catwalk collections. Finally, Willems is registered for a doctorate at the Faculty of Fine Arts, University College Ghent, in collaboration with the Department of Comparative Science of Culture at Ghent University, and the laboratory of Physical Medicine and Functional Morphology at the University of Antwerp. Her thesis involves interdisciplinary research and is entitled "Future Footwear," studying the latest developments in anatomy, ecology and design technology, and focusing on ethnic footwear in India and in Lapland as well as on contemporary high-fashion shoe design in Europe.

### Q What was the reason for your choice of PhD subject?
A My combined background led in 2005 to the start of a collection of footwear in conjunction with Toehold Artisans Collaborative in the south of India. TAC is a not-for-profit organization promoting the empowerment of rural women through entrepreneurial initiatives, with an emphasis on social and ecological accountability. The collections involve a combination of their traditional skills and new designs—traditionally they make Kolhapur footwear, which features a leather sole made out of vegetable-tanned buffalo hide, an instep band, and a toe strap or toe ring.

In September 2009 I started the PhD "Future Footwear," combining the study of the anatomy of feet, design methodology, and the ecological aspects of shoe design. The combination of my two main interests—anthropology and design—means that the research is intrinsically interdisciplinary. As well as the dissertation, my central objective is the artistic creation of a collection of anatomically, ecologically, and aesthetically designed footwear.

**Q Why feet and footwear?**
**A** I want to understand how people move and walk the way they do—with or without footwear. Broader questions that interest me are: Why do people make artifacts? And what is the relation between these artifacts and their environment?

**Q What is the importance of the connection between anatomy and design?**
**A** The past decade's footwear has been overengineered; athletic footwear has benefited from advanced technologies since the 1970s, yet injury statistics have not improved. Recently a lot of research has been done on the effects of walking barefoot or in minimal footwear, for example with no heel support. Insights from physical anthropology and from clinical work seem to indicate that when humans walked barefoot or in minimal footwear they suffered fewer injuries, although controlled studies are needed to test the various hypotheses. The footwear of the Sami people, which uses vegetable-tanned reindeer skins, may provide innovative insights in this field.

Fusing as it does exquisite craftsmanship with engineering, footwear design is quite unlike any other fashion discipline. Primarily worn to protect our feet, shoes also have a

*Traditional Kolhapur sandals are made from buffalo hide and are one of the most common types of footwear in India.*

# CASE STUDY: CATHERINE WILLEMS

different meaning. We choose our footwear according to our environment and we would no more wear rubber boots in the sun than sandals in the snow. And five-inch high heels are not worn because they are comfortable. In this way shoes will always relay important clues about our habitat and our ways of life. A comparison of such cultural and functional aspects of traditional footwear will help in understanding the process of creating and using footwear.

We fully analyze footwear from the anatomy of the feet to the symbolic and cultural aspects of the feet and footwear. The research covers both the biological/physical discipline in anthropology and the social/cultural discipline. The broader PhD project aims to develop a design toolbox for the efficient creation of future footwear. The ethnic footwear of the Sami and the Kolhapur footwear are exceptional because of the characteristics of the raw material used: reindeer hide and buffalo hide respectively. On a design level we move away from the standard view that form and substance are separate: we start from the material itself and its characteristics.

We study in detail the effect of footwear on the biomechanics of the foot by making a comparison between barefoot and shod walking, measuring how the biomechanics of the foot relate to the environment.

*Catherine tested, using numerous methods, the differences between walking barefoot and walking with shoes. It was important to do these studies outside of the laboratory environment.*

**Q Why India and Lapland?**

**A** Both examples have a long tradition of artisanal footwear production. The selection of the cases is based on surface, climate and the relation the community has with the environment, and the respective influence of these elements on the design of shoes. The research aims to gain insight into the practice of making footwear and the patterns of walking in a cross-cultural perspective.

Since we need comparable data the same setup will be used in India, in Lapland, and in Europe. In Lapland we will study reindeer hide and Sami boots, in India buffalo hide and Kolhapur chappals, and in Europe contemporary high-fashion footwear. The focus in each case is on the material used and its properties.

**Q What is the ultimate goal for you after you have completed your research?**

**A** First I want to answer the research questions. And in the end I hope the toolbox for footwear design is useful. I hope to be able to keep doing research on footwear and have the possibility to apply the results in collections.

**Q Is there any advice you can give a footwear design student?**

**A** My advice is to take the time to think about how form, function, and use relate to each other. What effect does this type of footwear have on our body? Why would someone want to wear that type of footwear? What effect does this type of footwear have on our environment—which materials do we use?

The term "design" does not only refer to the creation of form but also includes a method of thinking that combines and integrates other sciences. The research and creative work of the designer focuses on how we can analyze objects in our environment, and design and rebuild them for the benefit of general living and working conditions. Before you make a product, think about what design means in a global and dynamic society and how we can create sustainable products.

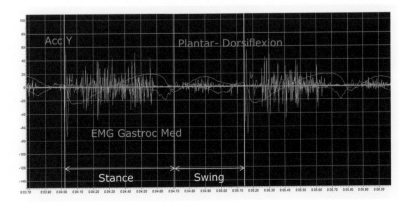

*After the results, which include gait and shock absorption, the biomechanical data will be analyzed and used for further study of the way we walk and use our feet.*

# CHAPTER 2
# SHOE BASICS

It is as important to understand the basic anatomy of the foot as it is to understand the inner makings of the shoe itself. A human foot is composed of more than a hundred different parts, while a shoe has to cover the foot and echo its movement with only a few main parts. The foot also has a direct connection to the well-being of the rest of the body and, therefore, the fitting and comfort of the shoe are important considerations of footwear design. In this chapter we will explore the basics of foot anatomy and take a detailed look at the composition of the shoe itself. We will also define most shoe styles and explain some basic terms to aid understanding of and communication within the industry.

# FOOT ANATOMY

The foot is one of the most complicated, most sensitive, and most used parts of the body. Our feet make up a small area, but they carry our whole weight and help us balance our bodies. They are under constant stress. We spend about 33 percent of our lives on our feet, either standing or walking. Made up of many moving parts, our feet are also full of nerve endings that communicate with the rest of the body. A well-designed shoe, therefore, should not only make you look good but should also be comfortable and promote efficient mobility.

To help ensure comfort, there are standard allowances that should be built into the shoe. "Toe spring," for example, is an essential allowance between the bottom of the toe of the shoe and the ground (the toe of the shoe tips up rather than sitting flat to the ground), used in order to accommodate the rocking motion of walking. Another important allowance is the space from the tip of the wearer's toes to the end of the shoe, called "overmeasure," generally $1/2$–$3/4$ in. This allows room for the foot's movement inside the shoe during the action of walking. The heel enclosure is also important in that it should correctly adjust to the ankle during movement (if too loose or too tight it may cause blisters). And the sole should be flexible enough to allow for walking. It is fair to say that most parts of the shoe are designed and tested to function not only while standing but, more especially, while walking. Shoes have a direct effect on foot health, and ultimately on the health of the whole body.

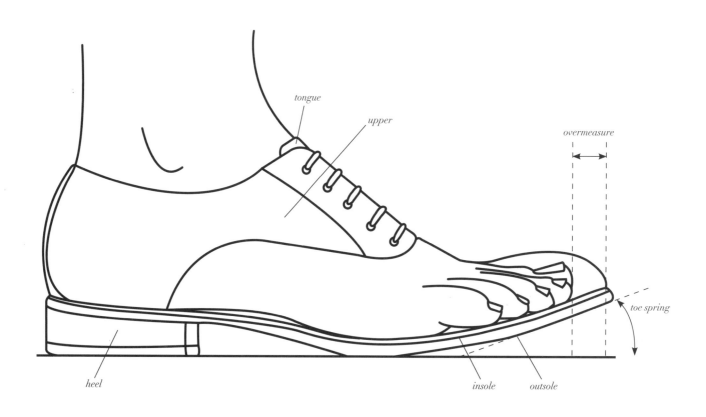

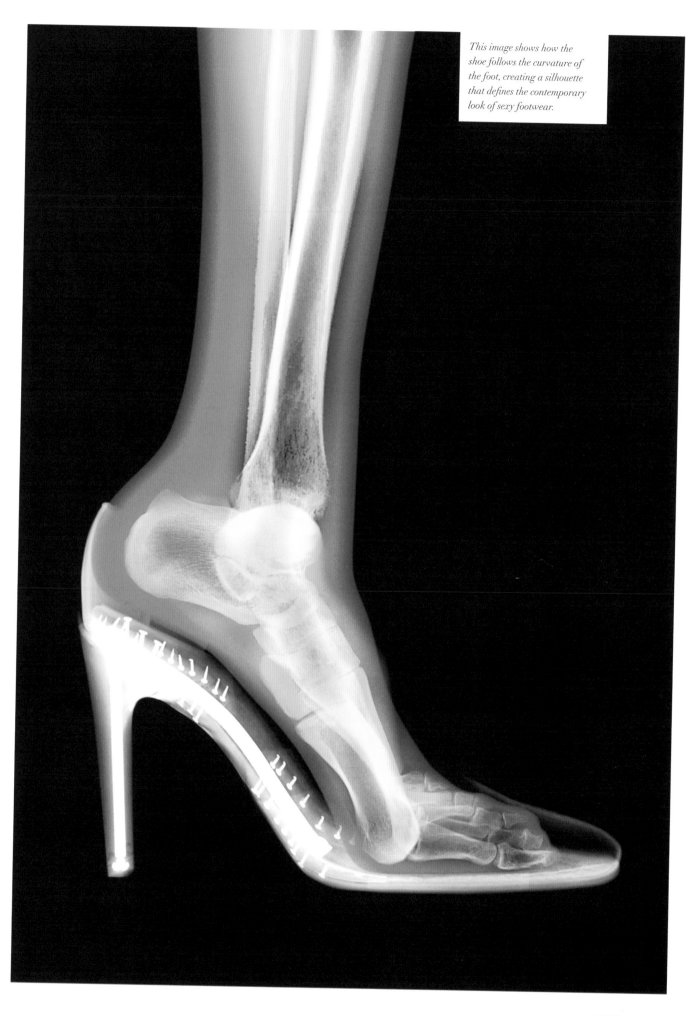

## ANATOMICAL MAKEUP OF THE FOOT

- 26 bones
- 33 joints
- Ligaments (tissues that connect bones)
- More than 100 muscles
- Tendons (fibrous connective tissue that connects muscle to bone)
- Blood vessels
- Nerves
- Skin, nails, and tissue

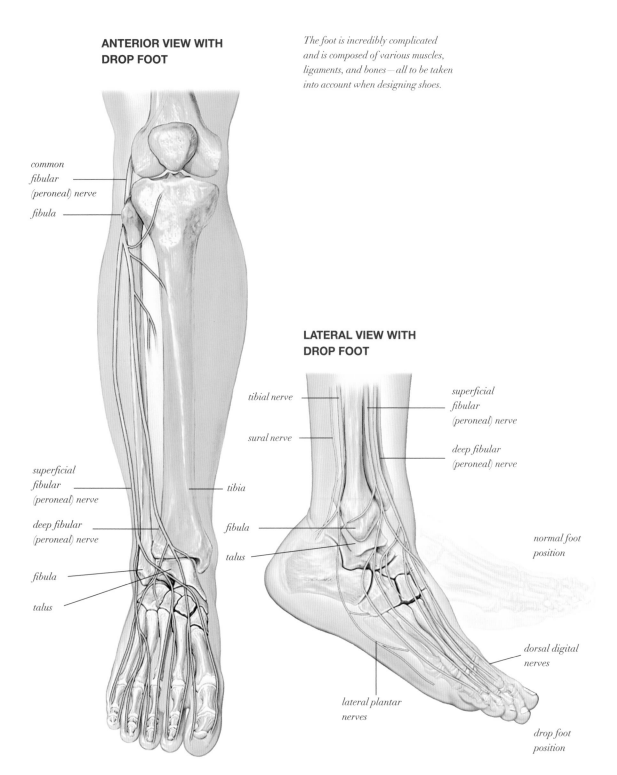

**ANTERIOR VIEW WITH DROP FOOT**

*The foot is incredibly complicated and is composed of various muscles, ligaments, and bones—all to be taken into account when designing shoes.*

common fibular (peroneal) nerve

fibula

superficial fibular (peroneal) nerve

deep fibular (peroneal) nerve

fibula

talus

tibia

fibula

talus

**LATERAL VIEW WITH DROP FOOT**

tibial nerve

sural nerve

superficial fibular (peroneal) nerve

deep fibular (peroneal) nerve

normal foot position

dorsal digital nerves

lateral plantar nerves

drop foot position

# BASIC SECTIONS OF THE FOOT

When referring to parts of the foot, a footwear designer should be aware that the foot consists of several basic sections:

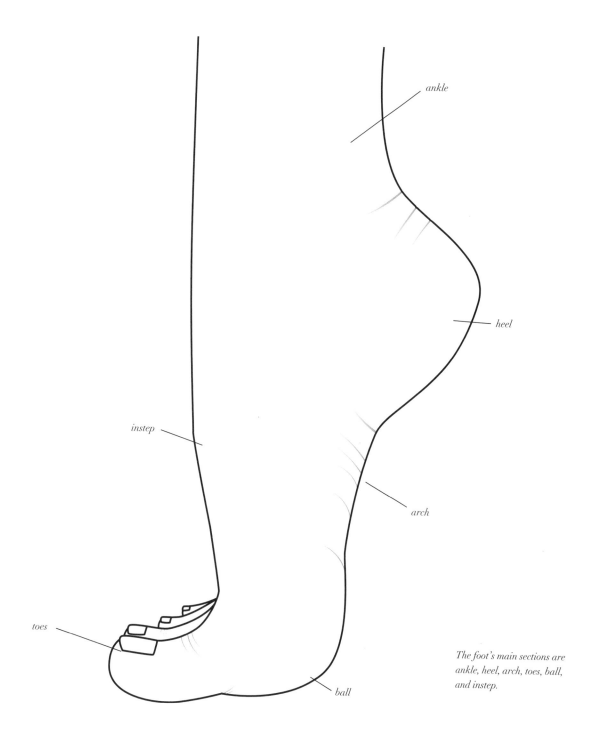

ankle

heel

instep

arch

toes

ball

*The foot's main sections are ankle, heel, arch, toes, ball, and instep.*

# SHOE ANATOMY

Shoes consist of considerably fewer main parts than the foot itself, but each is still designed to work with the movement of the foot. Before starting to design a shoe it is important to understand each of the component parts. It is also helpful to learn to identify each part by its industry standard name; this is especially useful when communicating your design ideas to factories or developers. The shoe is composed of numerous parts that are often manufactured independently but still need to work together as a dynamic whole. Heels and soles, for example, are usually made by experts in completely separate locations. Even the stitching of the upper sections (also known as "closing") can be outsourced. A shoe factory is merely the place where all these parts are assembled to produce a shoe. Generally speaking, factories do not produce any components or raw materials.

Following are definitions of the most important shoe components:

The **upper** is everything on the shoe above the sole. It is made up of pattern pieces that are sewn together. Common upper material is leather (mainly cowhide), but uppers can also be made of other materials such as textiles (e.g., synthetics, fabric, rubber).

The **lining** is important in keeping the internal parts of the upper in place by supporting it. Common lining materials include pigskin, calfskin, kidskin, and textiles.

A **toe box** helps to maintain the shape and height of the front end of the shoe. It is a piece of semirigid thermoplastic material that is heat-molded to the shape of the toe area. Finer shoes can have a toe box made of leather.

A **heel counter** helps in maintaining the shape of the heel cup area and in holding the heel of the foot in place. It is a piece of semi-rigid thermoplastic material. Finer shoes can have a heel counter made of leather.

The **sock lining** creates the surface that touches the bottom of the foot. It covers either the footbed or the insole (see below), and consists of a piece of leather or fabric. This is where the branding is commonly placed.

The **shank** acts as a supporting bridge between the heel and the ball of the foot. Attached to the insole board (see below), it is usually a steel strip but can also be made from nylon, wood, or even leather.

An **insole** provides structure and shape to the bottom of the shoe, its main function being a component to which the **upper** can be attached. It is made up of insole board and shank glued together. The **insole board** consists of cellulose board or a composite material.

An **outsole** is the bottom part of the shoe that touches the ground. Outsoles can be made from various materials depending on the price and the end use of the shoe. Leather, from bovine animals, is used for higher-end footwear. Materials such as natural crêpe rubber, resin rubber, polyurethane (PU), and vulcanized rubber are commonly used for soles (see p. 117).

The **heel** is a raised support of hard material, attached to the sole under the back part of the foot, usually made of hard plastic and covered in leather. Stacked leather, wood, or wood covered in leather are also occasionally used in higher-end footwear. The small plastic bottom tip of a woman's shoe-heel is called a **heel cap or heel tip**. It is designed to be easily replaced after wear and tear.

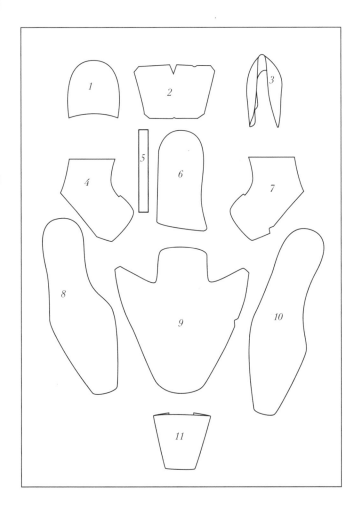

1  heel
2  counter lining
3  heel counter
4  quarter lining
5  shank
6  half sock lining
7  quarter lining
8  outsole
9  vamp lining
10  insole top view
11  toe box

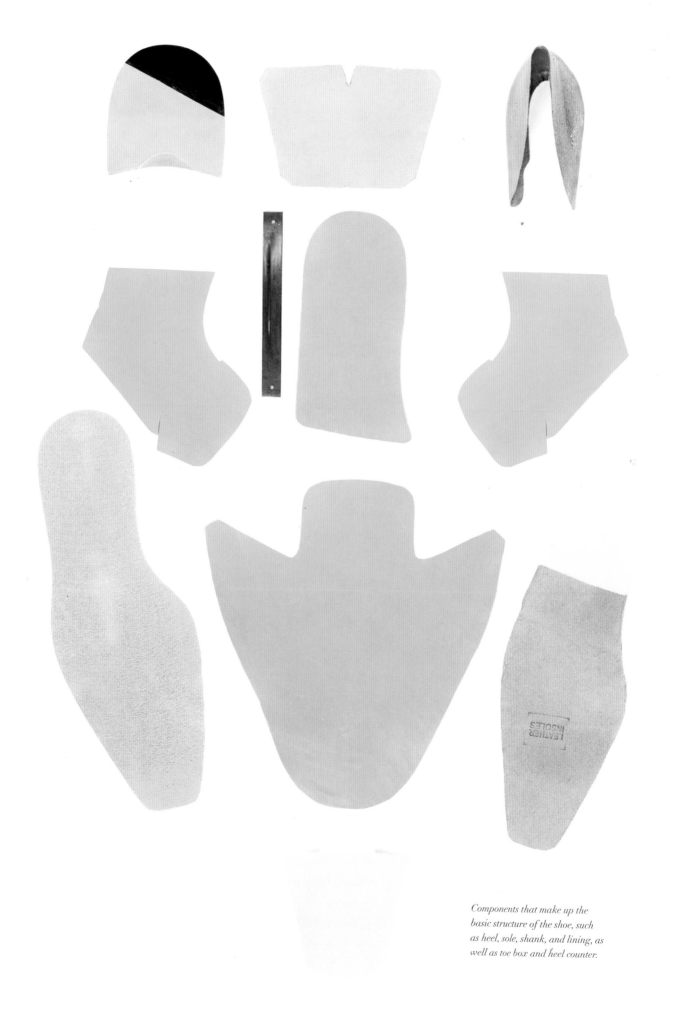

*Components that make up the basic structure of the shoe, such as heel, sole, shank, and lining, as well as toe box and heel counter.*

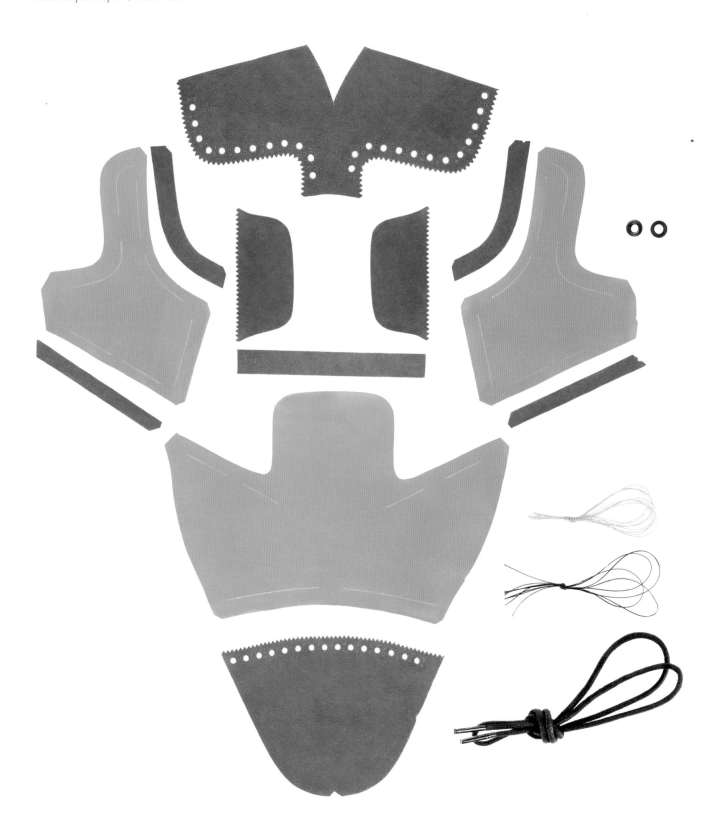

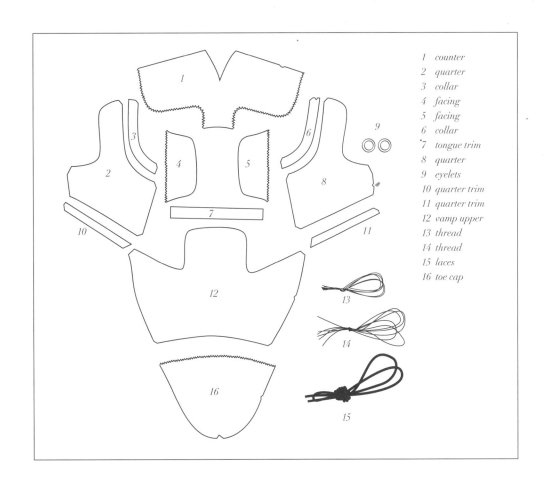

1  counter
2  quarter
3  collar
4  facing
5  facing
6  collar
7  tongue trim
8  quarter
9  eyelets
10  quarter trim
11  quarter trim
12  vamp upper
13  thread
14  thread
15  laces
16  toe cap

*When the components
and pattern pieces are
assembled the shoe is born.*

*Women's shoes use more delicate materials, hence the styles and methods used to make women's shoes are different to men's shoes.*

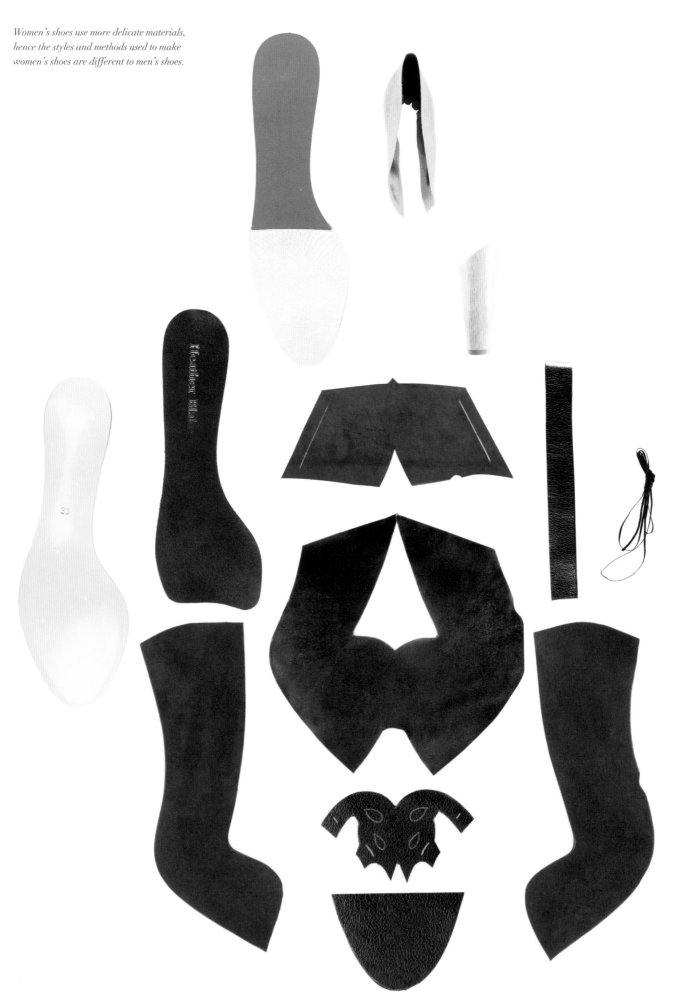

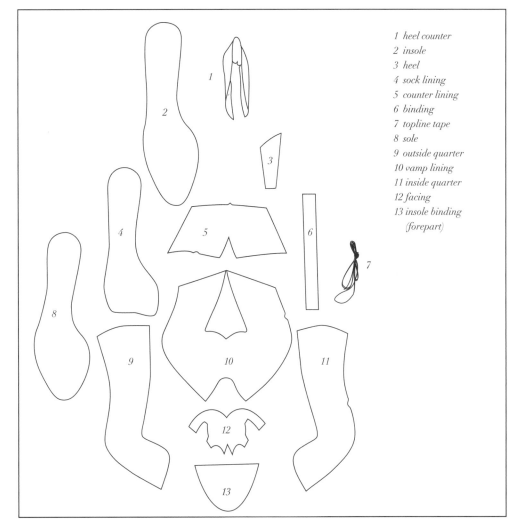

1 heel counter
2 insole
3 heel
4 sock lining
5 counter lining
6 binding
7 topline tape
8 sole
9 outside quarter
10 vamp lining
11 inside quarter
12 facing
13 insole binding
 (forepart)

Once the pattern pieces are sewn together and assembled with the sole and heel a shoe is produced. Women's shoes are made in different factories to men's since they require particular finesse and expertise. This shoe was designed by Heather Blake.

# THE LAST

The construction of a shoe begins with a last. A last is a stylized foot-shaped form that is used as a base upon which to build the shoe. However, note that the last should not be the *exact* shape and measurements of the foot. It is designed to fit inside the shoe, in the same way that a foot would fit inside a shoe, with allowances for movement. The last should also be designed to accommodate the shape of the heel and sole of the shoe. Last-making is a highly specialized skill because different types of footwear constructions, for example boots, sneakers, and moccasins, all require a specific last shape.

A last was traditionally made from wood, but more durable and recyclable polyethylene is now the preferred material in modern industrial shoemaking. Last-making is the most important part of shoemaking, since it determines the shape and fit of the shoe. Design development should start from the last: all the other components—most importantly the outsole and heel—are then designed to fit the last.

*Lasts come in a variety of shapes, as seen here in Sebastian Tarek's studio, and can be altered to fit one's foot perfectly.*

*The last shape becomes bulkier as more material is layered on it. These two images show clearly how the final shoe by Chau Har Lee (near left) is rounder and has more volume than the bare last (far left).*

*Different areas of the last have specific names.*

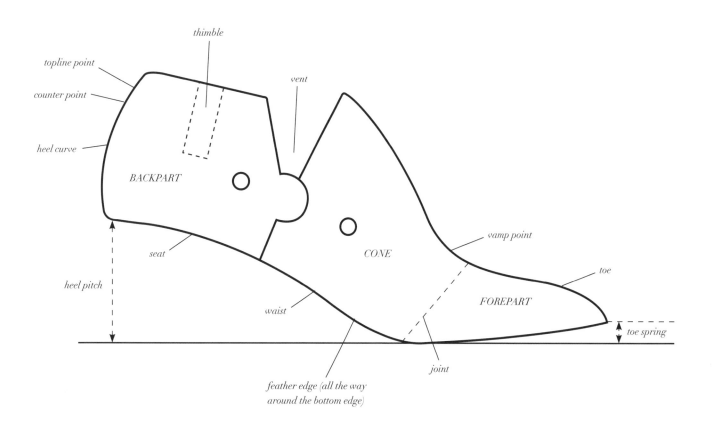

thimble

vent

topline point

counter point

heel curve

BACKPART

seat

heel pitch

waist

CONE

vamp point

toe

FOREPART

toe spring

joint

feather edge (all the way
around the bottom edge)

# PATTERNS

A pattern is an actual-size, two-dimensional representation of a last's three-dimensional surface. It is used to cut the upper material into the shapes required for the pieces of the shoe. "Pattern cutting" generally refers only to the upper. However, patterns are also needed for many other parts of the shoe (e.g., lining, insole, heel, sole). If you want to cover the heel with leather, for example, this piece requires a pattern in order for it to fit correctly onto the curves and angles of the heel.

A classic way of translating designs into patterns is the method of taping up a last in order to create a master pattern. Masking tape is attached to the last until it is completely covered and the shoe design is drawn on to the tape. The tape is then peeled off the last, flattened out, and used for making master patterns.

Another way to make patterns from your designs is to use a vacuum form. This is a plastic form that is heat-molded over the last and can then be drawn on, cut, and flattened into the pattern pieces desired. Some factories now require vacuum form designs in addition to drawings. Many companies, especially large-scale production factories, are also using computer programs to design footwear around preloaded, computerized 3-D lasts.

The art of pattern cutting is very precise, and takes many years to master. A mere fraction of an inch can make a big difference to the fit and comfort of a shoe. Since pattern cutting is a complicated process it is desirable to take additional classes to cover the importance of leaving allowances for seams and, ultimately, for lasting.

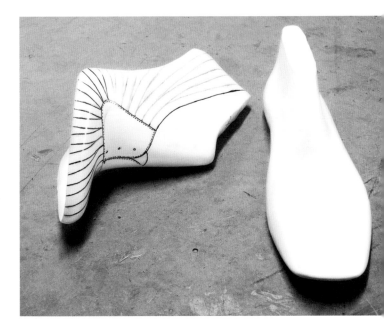

*Vacuum forms are widely used in the footwear industry. The designs are then taken from this three-dimensional surface to create patterns.*

*The upper consists of basic pattern pieces.*

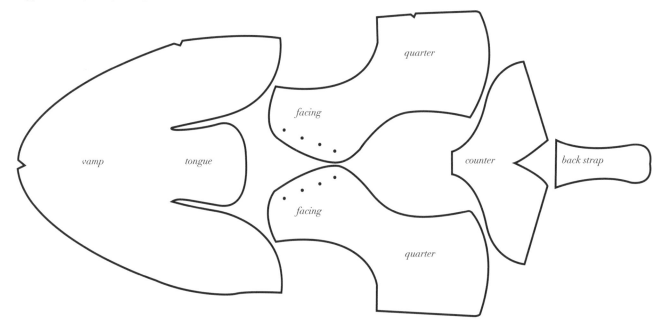

vamp

tongue

facing

facing

quarter

quarter

counter

back strap

*A last is often covered in masking tape to provide a surface that can be drawn upon, which is then flattened in order to create patterns.*

*Drawing on the tape-covered last will be your first step in creating a pattern.*

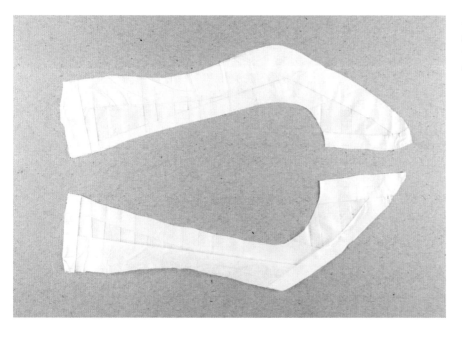

*Afterward, the initial patterns are peeled off the last and flattened for further pattern development.*

# MATERIALS USED IN THE SHOE INDUSTRY

The most suitable material for shoes, and perhaps the most commonly used, is leather. Leather is a by-product of the meat industry, obtained mainly from cattle. The characteristics of leather that make it ideal for shoes are durability, flexibility, and breathability. Before it can be used, the raw animal hide (or skin) must be tanned to prevent its putrefaction and to turn it into leather. Tanning has existed as an industry for thousands of years, and continues to be an integral part of the footwear and leather industries. All "skin" can be tanned, from frogs to chickens, but the three main categories in leather are "bovine" (hoofed animals such as cows and sheep), "ungulates" (even-toed animals such as pigs, sheep, and deer), and "exotics' (snakes, reptiles, and fish). There are two main tanning methods—chrome and vegetable tanning.

Eighty percent of leather is chrome-tanned. Chrome tanning involves the use of chromium salts and is a closely monitored industry in the West owing to the highly toxic waste that it produces. However, the benefits of chrome tanning over other methods—including the leather's resistance to the high heat involved in the industrial production of shoes—outweigh its disadvantages. It also performs well as far as coloring and consistency are concerned.

Vegetable-tanned leather is made using vegetable extracts and is mainly used for soles, belts, and luggage. It is also used in footwear, but is considered a niche market. Vegetable-tanned leather reacts to light more than chrome-tanned leather, but this is part of its character and can result in an interesting product; it also wears and ages beautifully. Many contemporary designers use part chrome-, part vegetable-tanned leather in order to obtain the benefits of both.

Textiles, both natural and synthetic, as well as other non-leather materials, are also used in the footwear industry. It is important to use material that is appropriate for footwear manufacturing. Textiles often have a backing applied to them so that they are durable enough to wear, and are able to stand the heat of the production process. Textile shoes are most often associated with summer, but can also be used in winter depending on the style and weight of the material.

*Aku Bäckström uses various interesting materials and finishes, such as felt and paint.*

*Textiles need to be the right weight and be "bleed-proof" in order to be used in footwear. This is due to higher wear and tear in shoes as compared to clothing.*

*Vegetable-tanned leather has warmer tones and does not come in bright color options. Made using vegetable extract in highly specialized tanneries, it is also more expensive.*

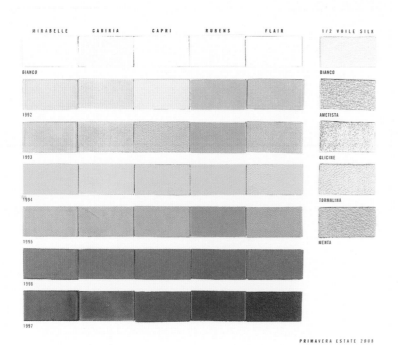

*Color will have a different look and feel depending on the underlying leather and material. This chrome-tanned color card shows the differences between finishes and types of leather.*

*Material mixes can provide interesting results as seen in this shoe, which uses leather and straw mixed with a sporty EVA (ethylene vinyl acetate) sole unit.*

# SHOE STYLES

The classic styles that apply to both men's and women's shoes are: Oxford, Derby, sandal, court shoe, boot, and mule. In contemporary shoe design, styles are reinterpreted and boundaries pushed daily. Following are some style definitions that are part of daily design terminology.

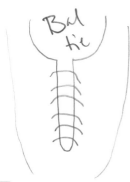

**Oxford:** The fore part of the shoe (vamp) is stitched on top of the side panels (quarters) of the shoe.

**Derby:** The quarters are stitched on top of the vamp.

*(also called blucher in USA)*

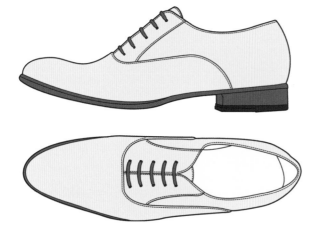

**Monk:** Derby with a strap crossing the top of the foot.

**Slip-on:** A laceless shoe that is designed to be put on and taken off easily.

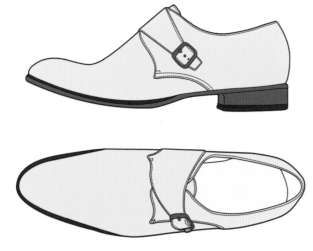

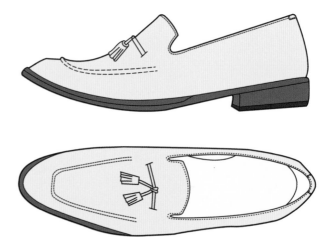

**Moccasin:** Refers to the ancient type of shoe construction where the bottom of the shoe is stretched around the sides of the foot and stitched to the "apron" on top.

**Jodhpur boot:** A short riding boot with an ankle strap.

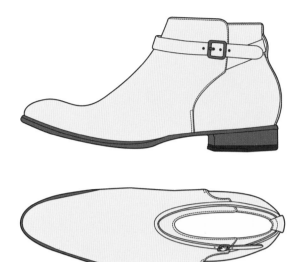

**Chelsea boot:** An ankle boot with side elastic gussets.

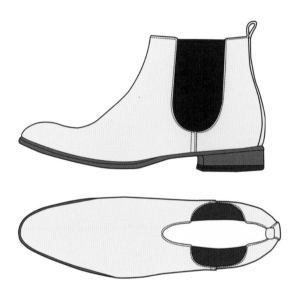

**Desert boot:** Traditionally unlined suede ankle boots that are side-stitched to a crêpe rubber sole.

*Desert boot is a blucher as well*

**Sneaker (or trainer):** A sport-inspired shoe that is generally designed for performance, but can also be used as a lifestyle fashion shoe.

**Boat shoe:** Originally a moccasin-style shoe made with a water-repellent hide, antislip outsoles, and side lacing. Nowadays any low-profile shoe with side lacing is referred to as a boat shoe.

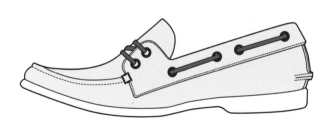

**Sandal:** Any shoe (high or low) that has the toes exposed.

**Mule:** An open-back shoe with no toes exposed.

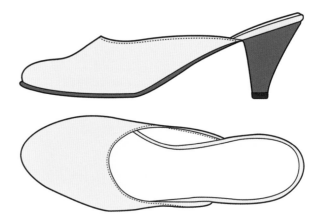

**D'Orsay:** A variation of the court shoe (see opposite page), having front and back uppers that do not meet. (There is also a semi-d'Orsay, where either the inside or the outside top edge dips down toward the sole to expose the side of the foot.)

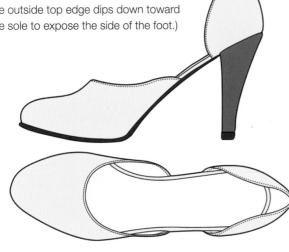

**Peep-toe:** A shoe that exposes a single toe.

**Platform:** The front part of the shoe is elevated as well as the heel.

**Mary Jane:** A court shoe with a single strap across the instep.

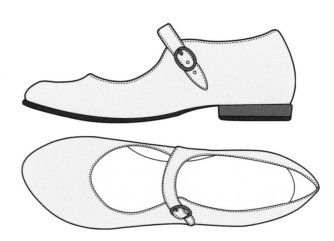

**Sling back:** An open-back shoe that has only a single back strap.

**Boot:** Any shoe with a higher ankle- or leg-covering section. Boots can be pull-on (i.e., with no openings) or fitted (e.g., with a zippered opening).

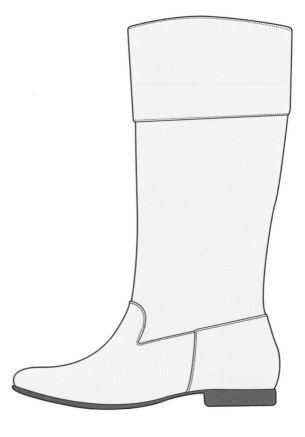

**Court shoe:** A closed top line (top edge) shoe.

**T-bar shoe:** A variation of the court shoe, having a single strap going up the vamp, attaching to another (somewhat perpendicular) strap, thereby forming a "T."

**Clog:** A shoe where the upper is generally stapled or nailed to a wooden sole.

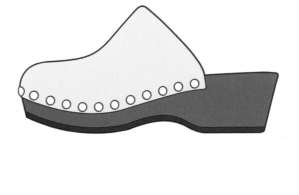

# CASE STUDY: SEBASTIAN TAREK

Australian-born Sebastian Tarek is a freelance bespoke shoemaker based in London, UK, and also teaches shoemaking courses. His work philosophy is to apply a contemporary aesthetic to the classic techniques used in the traditional British bespoke trade. Sebastian was born in 1977, making him relatively young in the bespoke shoe world where the average age is over sixty. He currently works with two of the oldest surviving shoemakers in London—George Cleverley & Co. and James Taylor & Son—as well as his own eponymous bespoke service.

### Q Why did you choose this career?
**A** My career has evolved out of an initial interest in fashion and a fascination with how an object as functional as a shoe fits within a field that can be so decorative. Handmade and bespoke shoes take the idea even further, and the foot itself becomes the template for something genuinely sculptural. The need to solve the problems of how to integrate the foot with the way a shoe can and should look is a fantastic challenge.

### Q Where/how did you train?
**A** I started off in vocational study, in both the UK and Australia, and then found opportunities for on-the-job training as well as private projects in which to develop a greater understanding of practices and my own techniques.

### Q What is the best part of your job?
**A** Facing challenges, and working out how to address problems such as how to create beautiful shapes for the feet I am fitting. Working on developing specific skills and honing techniques that have been learned recently, so are fresh; as well as constantly refining the age-old techniques that go with classic handmade shoemaking. Interacting with people to create something both beautiful and functional. And being my own boss, so working in an unrestrictive environment that I have created myself. I get to be responsible for how I develop my career, which is a fantastic challenge in itself.

### Q What is the worst?
**A** The physical aspect of working with techniques completely devoid of machinery is taxing on the body sometimes—though it gives a great sense of achievement to finish a hard day at the office with sore limbs knowing that you have done a good day's work.

### Q What is important in shoemaking?
**A** Application to the task at hand and making sure it is done properly, no matter how long it takes. Patience is probably the greatest virtue in this field. Realizing details, and understanding how it is often the sum total of these details that makes the difference between a pair of shoes and a beautiful pair of shoes.

### Q What materials do you prefer working with?
**A** I love the malleability and diversity of vegetable-tanned leathers—the character that these ancient tanning techniques

*Sebastian applying adhesive to the bottom of the shoe; this preparation is only a fraction of the time-consuming process.*

give to the leather. I work a lot with kangaroo and enjoy all the properties that veg-tanned kangaroo provides. I enjoy working with skins with a depth of color and an obvious character that will develop with age. I have always loved good box calf in the brown and tan colors that are common in the London bespoke trade. And as a vegetarian I also regularly find myself working with different canvases and cotton. Waxed canvas and heavy cotton drills operate completely differently from leather but are required to serve the same function.

**Q What is a typical day for you?**

**A** Into the studio early so as not to end up leaving close to midnight. My particular field requires long days and sometimes the processes used require you to stay and finish something no matter what, or risk having to redo the whole thing. As most of my time is taken up with the arduous process of stitching soles on by hand I will usually start off with the gentler things such as making my thread, which is wound linen burnished into a strong thread with tar and beeswax. I have to get soles prepped, cut to shape, and skived in appropriate places and soaked and mellowed to allow them to take shape over the last. I like to have all these things done by lunchtime so that I can come back, sit in my chair, and take on the task of stitching on the welts and soles, so that the whole shoe can dry overnight, to be rasped into shape the next day and have the edges set.

**Q What career advice could you give to a student who wanted to become a bespoke maker?**

**A** To find someone whose advice you trust in the industry. I had a very naive idea of what a shoemaker did when I first started. It has largely been through the relationships I formed with people whom I worked with that the skills and techniques I cherish were acquired. Try and find something that you can work on at home or outside of a job to help develop key skills like lasting, so finding a style of shoe that you can work on that doesn't involve machines too much is a good start. There are a surprising amount of them that you can play around with and have some fun. Be prepared to work hard, it is a tough job and you have to get yourself in the right shape to do it. Your hands have to become like shovels before you can make enough work in a day without them hurting, so be prepared to suffer a little bit. But it's worth it.

**Q Where do you see yourself in the future?**

**A** Doing exactly what I'm doing now. I would like to develop a bigger private client base and be able to work more on the commissions that I have the greatest input with, but I love the flexibility of working for the old firms as well, and the opportunity of working with amazing craftspeople. I would never give it up.

*Welting is what makes handmade shoes worth the investment, as demonstrated in this image.*

# CHAPTER 3
# RESEARCH

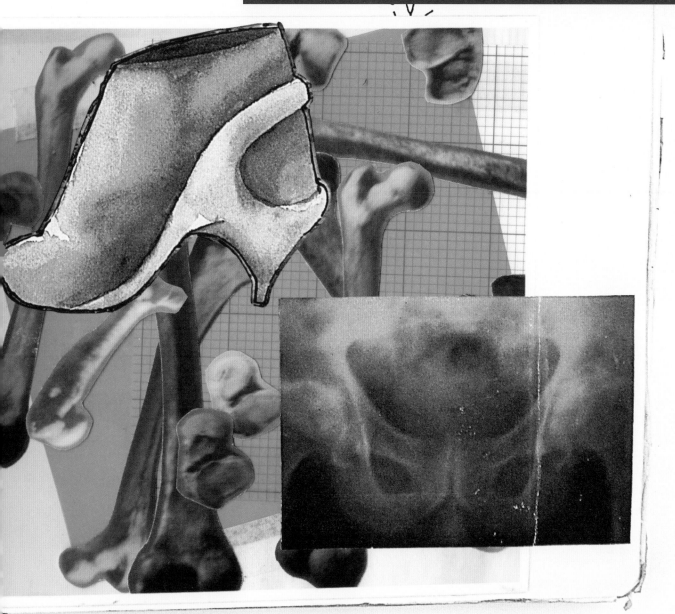

**Research is an important part of the design process. It is an excellent way of investigating a subject in depth, and of finding new ideas with which to work—your research might throw up ideas for colors, details, even a name for your collection. It will also serve as a solid base for your collection, giving it a theme and a clear look. Your aim should be to develop a well-researched theme that will add richness and scope to your collection, and will be invaluable throughout every stage of design, up to and including selling and marketing your product.**

Your audience is always interested in where your ideas come from, and in your thought processes. Research helps you to put together a collection that derives from a single pool of ideas, thus creating a unifying story for all your pieces. Some designers take the research and theme and extend it from shoe design development all the way to printing the shoebox tissue paper, designing the invitation to the launch, and general marketing. Designers have their own systems for researching and designing; there is no single correct way to do it. However, this chapter will give you some guidelines, something on which to base your own system.

There are three essential parts to research: inspiration, investigation, and process. The theme, or dominant unifying idea, will initially emerge out of the inspiration stage. During the investigation your theme will be refined through further exploration. In the process stage you will be working more with the practical translation of research ideas—in other words, how they will be applied to your final collection.

The result of your research will be a sketchbook and a mood board. Designers often have a theme wall in their studio, whereas most students use inspirational sketchbooks. A sketchbook is a powerful tool to use for your collection, and a good way to archive visual information for future reference. There is no set time frame for when you should start to create your sketchbook, but generally you would start jotting down early ideas toward the end of the inspiration phase or the beginning of the investigation stage. The compilation of the sketchbook should happen throughout the process stage, with completion before the final collection is designed. A mood or theme board is a summary of your research and acts as an introduction to your collection. The mood board can be constructed and finalized during the process stage.

In addition to your sketchbook and mood board, color should play an important part in your research. The final color palette can be added to your mood board or kept on a separate color board.

Ultimately your research process should be enjoyable.

# INSPIRATION

For some, finding inspiration is easy, for others less so. But where does one find inspiration? Inspiration can come from anything that surrounds you. The things that inspire you about life in general are a good starting point for research: for example, does your personal history and culture inspire you? Ideally inspiration should come from personal observation, and should not be borrowed from fashion magazines or other designers' work. Your audience wants to know your story and where your ideas come from. Inspiration might be found in museums, galleries, exhibitions, architecture, books, cinema, street culture… or life in general. The theme for your collection will come from your inspiration.

Theme is essential to your storytelling. The theme does not necessarily have to be a single idea, but can be a mixture of references that will make it even more appealing. A good theme is something that will inspire you to develop compelling ideas for silhouette, volume, and color—all the things that make your collection interesting. A theme really can be anything; the important part is how you use it and what you make of it. "Feathers" is not a good theme because it is highly specific. A story about flying, perhaps inspired by a book or a movie, would be more interesting; it could be broken down later and "feathers" could be explored as part of your research.

Take, for example, three completely different examples of themes for student research: blueberry pie, bones, and Black Beauty. One student was inspired by blueberry pie. Not the most obvious source of inspiration. However, in her research she dissected the subject completely. What is the history of pie? What is it made

of, what is the chemical composition of the ingredients? What makes blueberries blue? This is a good example if you want to stick to a limited subject, and expand your research around it. Another student was inspired by an exhibition in a medical history museum—specifically, the bones and bone structures of the human body. This research led to structural research ideas surrounding architectural concepts of scaffolding. The subject matter automatically led the research in a more technical direction, quite different from the more quirky blueberry pie research. For a third student the story of Black Beauty led to rich and plentiful research on horses, saddle-making, and many other ideas surrounding riding.

You can choose any theme you like, but your research will be richer if you focus on broader concepts at first, then focus in on something more specific at the next stage.

## INSPIRATION IS ABOUT:

### Curiosity
Designers are naturally curious about the world surrounding them. You are constantly bombarded by information wherever you go: posters, magazines, newspapers, TV, and the Internet. Everybody wants to shape your opinion. But it is important not to be overly influenced by others' opinions, and instead focus only on the content and develop your own views. What you really need to look for is information—preferably new information. Consider how this information makes you feel. Things that are not part of your everyday life can be very inspirational.

*The straw and its use in Diego Oliveira Reis's research provides an inspirational cross-cultural journey through material possibilities.*

*Diego Oliveira Reis's research has good, clear material image references that create a base for further raw material experimentation.*

*Inspiration can come from surprising things, as proved by Jin Hong's "blueberry pie" theme. Simply redrawing your subject may bring new depth to your research.*

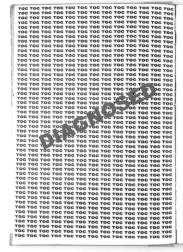

*Inspiration and research can be very personal; this theme was based on scans of Diego Oliveira Reis's own brain.*

## Thoughts

Inspiration can come from simply thinking or daydreaming. Let your imagination take your thoughts and go with it. Do a little bit of "brain sailing"—a softer version of brainstorming. Ideas should start off slowly, and come to you steadily—let your brain do the hard work, while your body is relaxing. All you need to do is write down the ideas that keep coming in. It is also good sometimes to pull yourself away from your work for a while.

## Concepts

Inspiration can spring from a conceptual approach. There are many concepts in the world that will not be developed into a final product. A building that will never be built, or a project that is still years away from realization. It is equally acceptable for a shoe designer to work on a conceptual level where, perhaps, comfort and mobility are not the prime considerations. You can look at the shoe as a design object—something you can start your design from. A whole collection can spring from a single conceptual piece.

## Movements

Artistic, philosophical, political—the world is full of new ideas and ideological movements. One good example is the notion of sustainable living, which has given rise to innumerable design ideas over the last ten years or so. Many fashion and footwear designers are inspired by the movement and are looking for ways to create products that are attractive to wear but also ecologically sound.

*Benjamin John Hall's collection entitled Party Politics demonstrates how ideas can come from things we deal with in our daily lives.*

*Helen Furber has created a luxury ecological concept that uses a unique glueless modular construction. This concept provides a platform for new production possibilities.*

## Free thinking

You might find that your research takes you in a new direction. Do not let your original theme limit you and your thought process. If you find an exciting new direction, idea, or path, go for it! Your initial inspiration might be something historical, such as armor, that will take you to study the mechanics of machinery. This could, in turn, lead you into automobiles, or in a different direction altogether. You could abandon armor, take that new path of cars, and totally immerse yourself in that research. Alternatively, you might cross-reference ideas but stay with the original theme.

## Marginal influences

Feel free to go right to the fringes of the thought process. Ideas can come from unexpected sources and areas of thought where usually you might not dare to go. You should not be afraid of seeking inspiration and solutions from subcultures or cultures that might make you a bit uncomfortable. For example, in exploring ideas on the manipulation of leather you could look into body modification such as tribal scarring, tattoos, and piercing.

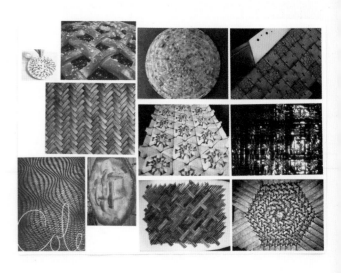

*Jin Hong's research shows how inspiration can come from the most unusual ideas – in this instance, blueberry pie.*

*Diego Oliveira Reis's theme based on the Ballets Russes shows such detail in the costumes. Archival images can provide great color and material inspiration as well.*

*Grace Zhong's inspiration came from Black Beauty. This led her to study all the bridle details, such as straps and harnesses as well as metal parts and horse shoes. When you are researching a theme you can let it take you in unexpected directions.*

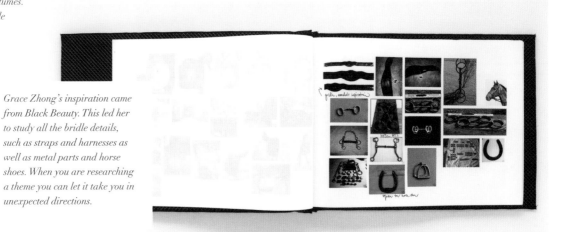

# INVESTIGATION

Investigation is the actual gathering of information about the theme that emerged as a result of the inspiration stage. This is also when your sketchbook really starts to develop. Investigative action is broken down into two types of research: primary and secondary. Primary research is when you personally gather the information or replicate it—perhaps a sketch that you have drawn in a museum or a photograph that you have taken. When collecting information, especially sketching, you get a real sense of personal discovery. Secondary research is when someone else has done the work, such as if you are using existing research that appears on the Internet or in books and magazines. It is easy nowadays to find images and visuals on the Internet using numerous search engines. But you should not rely solely on Internet-based research: a well-balanced mix of primary and secondary research will produce a more satisfying result.

When you combine primary and secondary research you create a solid platform based on outside sources mixed in with personal references. The bulk of the research will inevitably be about you and your views, since you are using your personal editorial skills to gather all the information. At this stage it is important not to think too far ahead. Do not limit your research options by thinking literally about a shoe—focusing on a chair leg that would make a nice heel, for example—as this will needlessly limit your creative thinking process. You will develop design ideas later from the research. At this stage your sketchbook can begin to show some very early and distant references to footwear, but try to stay away from the obvious. Sometimes the most obvious choice does work, but that decision can be made nearer the end of the creative process.

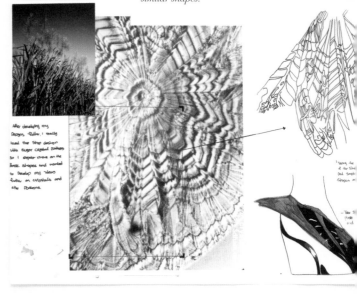

*Jin Hong's blueberry pie theme took the research deeper by studying sugar cane, the crystal structure of sugar, and other similar shapes.*

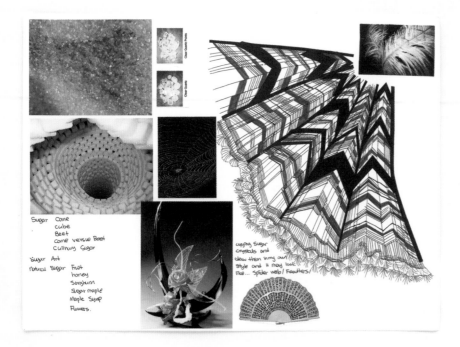

*Sugar and its different forms can be used to provide inspiration for patterns, color, and texture, as seen here in Jin Hong's research.*

## INVESTIGATION IS ABOUT:

### Gathering information

The investigative action involves sketching, photographing, photocopying, tearing pages out of magazines, and collecting material references such as leather swatches, textile references, and color information. What you want to do is make your sketchbook as inspirational as possible. At this stage just gather the information; perform an edit of the material at a later stage.

*Art Nouveau imagery inspired Diego Oliveira Reis to create a three-dimensional expression directly onto the last; this can then be used to draw further variations.*

*Paper is a great material to use for draping. It is cheap, easy to cut, and easy to attach to the last. Take a photo of your draping and use it as a basis for your drawings and designs, as done here by Diego Oliveira Reis.*

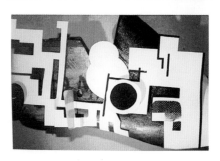 

*These paper-cut drapes by Diego Oliveira Reis were inspired by the Ballets Russes and the art of its time. It is important to take pictures of the draped lasts, as it is the best way to archive your research information.*

## Experiencing a theme

To go deeper into the theme, try to experience it. If your research theme is "magic," for example, try to go and see a performance, or learn a few tricks yourself. It is important to get to know your subject better. Seek out places where you can get more information on the theme. Can you find a person who is an expert in the field? It is surprising how many specialists and academics will answer professional e-mails relating to their subject. Is there something they can suggest or even demonstrate that relates to your research?

## Not setting limits

Set no limits for yourself or your work. Try not to work under strict time limits (which can be difficult in a seasonal fashion environment), but rather let it all happen naturally. If your inspiration takes you to an unrelated field, don't stop yourself! The more information you gather and the more varied the sources, the better.

## Exploring different paths

You might be inspired to go in another direction, which could be even more inspirational. It is perfectly acceptable to mix ideas and directions. If your research is about wind instruments this may lead to research into accordions, which might lead to the study of collapsing structures, and so on. It is actually healthy to explore various paths and find new ways. You can connect all the points, or eliminate some of the dead ends, later.

## Documenting ideas

Always keep all materials that you have produced. Archiving information is about keeping track of your journey. This does not mean, however, that all the found material should be compiled in your sketchbook. It is better to edit your sketchbook, and keep the rest of the research material separately archived. Later it will make a great personal reference library.

## Gathering visual details

Research is about images and visually interesting details. The visual details can come from primary or secondary research. Whenever you do two- or three-dimensional experimentation or research with different materials, take photographs of your process and use those as documents from which to draw inspiration.

You can gather information (photographs, sketches, notes, etc.) from museums, galleries, art and architecture, the street (street language, street dress), youth movements, subcultures, costume history, cultural heritage, historical archives, libraries, associations, foundations—the sources are truly limitless.

## Museums

Museums provide incredibly rich sources for research, containing as they do all sorts of historical references to the achievements of man, whether archaeological, artistic, or medical, for example. Museums also provide a good platform for hunting down details and color. Many museums do not allow photography, so be prepared with a notebook and pencil (some do not allow ink pens). You can take notes and make quick sketches of what you see, and fill in the details later from memory. It is not a problem

*Wellcome Trust's Wellcome Collection, London, is a medical history museum that has a changing exhibition space as well as a permanent collection. The museum offers many historical and contemporary sources of inspiration.*

if you do not remember all the details. Let your creativity and imagination fill in the missing parts, allowing the sketches to become a little more personal.

## Contemporary art

Contemporary art offers wonderfully fresh views—the opportunity to develop countless creative ideas and new directions of thought awaits you. Galleries are also an ideal environment from which to acquire strong color stories. International art shows such as the Venice Biennale, Art Basel Miami Beach, and Frieze Art offer limitless opportunities and sources of inspiration. Contemporary art is not seasonal: these works are personal stories that should trigger your thinking process.

## Architecture

Structures, surfaces, volumes, and uses of materials can give you many ideas about how to develop similar techniques in your shoe designs, albeit on a smaller scale. After all, a piece of footwear is a small object that has been designed to support a relatively large amount of weight. It is not impossible to imagine a shoe compared to a small building.

*A contemporary arts environment offers wonderful inspiration for concept, color, and material use.*

*Architectural concepts and ideas will provide solutions to many design issues. You can always take these grander-scale ideas and modify them for use in footwear. These concept boards are by Michala Allen.*

## Street culture

The street can be a great source of new ideas. This is especially true in the fashion capitals of the world, where people really like to express their individuality. There are numerous street fashion blogs that include photographs of people and their individual styles from all over the world. Street blogs often document new and unexpected ways of wearing something, which could inspire new solutions for your designs. They can also help you identify the person who would wear your shoes and help you with styling and presentation ideas. It is also important to add a human element to your research and design process. Adding references to the body will bring a more complete feeling to your research and ultimately to the collection.

*Streetwear blogs are a good source of ideas from the end user, including their use of styling shoes in conjunction with clothing.*

## Subcultures and youth movements

The hippies of the 1960s, the punks of the 1970s, and the new romantics of the 1980s were some of the great fashion influences of the past decades. Sandals were the footwear of choice for hippies, with more militant combat boots and brothel creepers for punk, and pixie boots to go with the flamboyant looks of the 1980s. Fetish groups, Internet gamers, burlesque, goths, and numerous others, all continue to flourish and give us fresh ideas. There are new cultures and subcultures evolving all the time, with new points of view filtering out to the design community.

## Costume history and cultural heritage

Different cultures and their costume history can provide a rewarding pool of ideas for investigation. You might also be inspired by different craft techniques and the rich heritage that different cultures can offer. It does not matter if your theme is something futuristic or sporty—you might still learn a specific method of weaving or embroidery from an ethnic cultural heritage.

## Libraries and archives

Libraries are used less and less frequently nowadays. Yet many libraries contain treasure troves of visual information in vast collections of out-of-print books. Do not forget that museums and collections often have private research libraries. You might need photo ID and an appointment for admission, but the discoveries to be made can be well worth the effort. Recent graduate Diego Oliveira Reis's research of his native Brazilian culture in the Victoria and Albert Museum led to the incorporation of images of early immigrants in his collage work.

*The coverage in streetwear blogs is not only about what people wear but also how they wear it.*

# THE PROCESS

The process is the use to which you put the research. It is about digesting the information you have collected, with a focus on a few main directions and ideas. It is basically the product development stage of your research. You will now take all the material and start being more focused. This is the stage when you finalize your sketchbook. You will go through the selection process, and start putting into your sketchbook only things that matter. In this part you will also start experimenting with materials, textures, and colors. Start thinking about very early design ideas and making connections. It is also important to start thinking three-dimensionally: you are, after all, designing an object. A great way to explore dimensionality is to begin experimenting with paper and masking tape, draping directly on to the last. Taking pictures of your experiments can add an excellent personal dimension to your sketchbook.

## PROCESS IS ABOUT:

### Exploring materials and color

Material experimentation is very important in order to glean new ideas for your collection. You can manipulate leather in numerous different ways—by drawing directly on to it, by wetting and molding it, by dying it, by burning it. You can equally be inspired by many other materials that are not used in the footwear industry. Hardware stores are treasure troves of new materials. Many building materials, including tapes, wallpapers, and flooring, can provide great new directions while acting as substitutes for leather in your research. You can also get color reference and surface ideas from this type of research. Again, document the process either by drawing the material, taking photographs, or adding the less bulky swatches to your sketchbook.

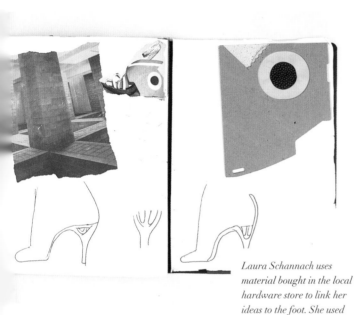

*Laura Schannach uses material bought in the local hardware store to link her ideas to the foot. She used cut-up vacuum cleaner bags to create the drapes.*

*Diego Oliveira Reis uses leather to imitate some of the details found in his research. At this point you should start thinking more about how your research could work in the realm of shoes.*

*Bridlework and hardware provide great inspirational ideas for Grace Zhong's work based on Black Beauty. The images are a good mixture of primary and secondary research.*

## Filtering

Filtering is about editing and selecting items from your research to build a sensible whole and using only references that matter. You will need to take a good look at all the material you have gathered and really consider it. Ask yourself: Does your research really relate to your work? Is there a clear connection, or do you really have to work to demonstrate a connection? If the connection needs extensive explanation—leave it out.

## Improvisation

Take your design theme and bring in ideas that are unexpected. You can embody your design ideas with materials that relate to your theme, like Diego Oliveira Reis's inspirational shoe model that was made using X-rays of his own body. Don't be afraid to improvise and use new materials. You can even use digital modification of images to obtain new shapes and volumes. Use whatever you can get your hands on to provide ideas and references for your research. You can try and express the designs with any material—looking at how they cross over from flat drawings to three-dimensional models.

## Drawing initial ideas

Starting to sketch early design ideas will help you stay focused on what you ultimately plan on doing—designing a footwear collection. The sketchbook should have a slow development of general ideas, maybe with some detail. Drawing is an effective way to link images and ideas together and bring your personal handwriting to your sketchbook. The type of drawing or illustrations you do is not important. What is important is that they show the initial ideas, since you will develop designs and specific details after the bulk of the research work is done.

*Diego Oliveira Reis took his own brain scan and used this very personal theme to create this three-dimensional, inspirational "X-ray" shoe.*

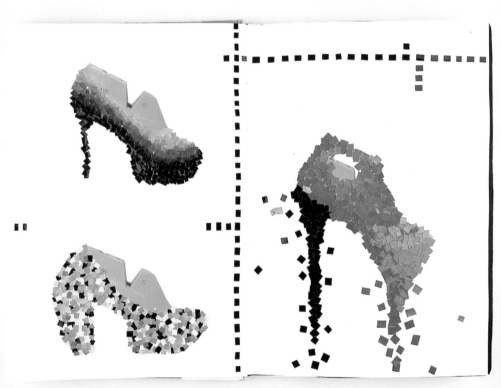

*A collage of materials placed directly on the last or foot shape will let your imagination fly; there are limitless new volumes and shapes to be found, as demonstrated in Diego Oliveira Reis's designs.*

# COMPILING A SKETCHBOOK

The more research you do, the closer to and more familiar with your theme you will become. Your research should form the basis of the sketchbook. The sketchbook is not only a book of sketches, but should be a well-researched book of inspirational ideas that you can use to design collections and which also presents an interesting mix of primary and secondary research. Your sketchbook will help you during the design development stage and will be a point of reference when putting your collection together.

**1.** Buy a blank sketchbook of medium-weight paper. It must be thick enough to absorb markers or other rendering materials, and not allow the colors to bleed through the paper. You can make your own book if you prefer, or create your own way to express your research. However, a traditional sketchbook is the easiest way to get started.

**2.** Fill the beginning of the sketchbook with inspirational visuals such as photos, pictures from catalogs or magazines, printouts of digital research, or photocopied research. Leave blank spaces next to the images for drawing. Drawing details you see in these images is the best way to really focus on what you see. By redrawing your subject matter you can go deeper into it. You can redraw either the full image or just a detail that you find interesting.

*Laura Schannach's exploration of shape comes from bones that are first redrawn, and then reproduced on a shoe shape to provide a base for further shape development.*

*A simple sketchbook with no branding is the best and least distracting. Ringbound sketchbooks allow a little more flexibility when working on pages, especially if sticking in bulkier material.*

**Tip**

It is best to start working on the sketchbook during the early stages of your research, and fully delve into it during the final process. You can start putting down some brief ideas as early as the inspiration stage, but these should really just pave the way for the more focused research later.

**Tip**

The sketchbook should show a roughly chronological development of your ideas. Do not go too far back into your book and "fill in the blanks" or try to prettify it. It is not about making a beautiful scrapbook but is, rather, a visual account of your progression.

*Diego Oliveira Reis gets useful references from costume history—in particular from the details, closures, and techniques that are no longer in use today.*

**Tip**

If you use images from magazines, make sure you take out any reference to the publication itself, including page numbers or any text from the feature, as this can distract from the actual image you want to use. It is also important to keep notes (but not necessarily to annotate each image) about where the images came from. Who are you referencing? What is the name of the artist? The photographer? The architect? The designer?

Drawings in your sketchbook should link the images you have to your theme, and more specifically to footwear. Through your drawing you can also bring personal "handwriting" to your sketchbook.

**3.** Start to add other materials to your sketchbook. Try imitating some textural (surface) ideas from your research—for example, if you find a basket inspirational try to imitate the weave with paper or rope and insert the results in the book. Learn more about the ideas by simply repeating some of them. Your sketchbook should also contain swatches and references to different materials, such as leather or textiles. Slowly start filling in the blank spaces of your sketchbook, to make it visually interesting and inspiring. Use your editorial eye; it is not necessary to fill and decorate every page. A blank page can sometimes be a welcome pause next to a strong image.

**4.** While you are compiling your sketchbook add some subtle references to shoes and footwear. These could include a few silhouette ideas, or some details showing how an idea could be developed in a shoe. You can either draw directly next to or on top of your visuals, or use tracing paper that you can then stick in the sketchbook.

**Tip**
The sketchbook does not have to be ornamental or systematic. Just keep building up as much information as you need. Use adhesive tape, staples, and so on to add initial drawings and footwear references.

After visual references, try to imitate surfaces with your own materials. Diego Oliveira Reis uses suede and textiles to bring more textural interest to the research.

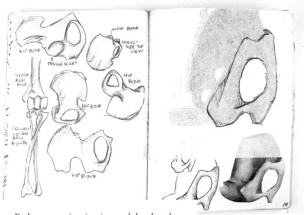

Redraw your inspiration and develop the shapes further. Laura Schannach draws a new shape on transparent paper, which is then placed over a drawn shape, giving it new dimensionality.

Sometimes color images mixed with material references that relate to your theme will add interest and serve as inspiration for the development of designs. Here is a spread from Diego Oliveira Reis's sketchbook.

## RESEARCH GATHERING EXERCISES

Go to a museum or a park, or simply look around your neighborhood, and sketch 50 details that you like. Once again, it is important not to jump ahead by thinking about how you might use these details in your shoe design: that will be part of the development process later. Focus on details for now. The 50 sketches can be very quick—visual notes to remind you of what you have seen. Back at your desk, start adding a little bit more detail and complete the drawings from memory. Don't worry if you don't remember all the particulars. In finishing the drawings from memory you are already tapping into your inspiration, and making the sketches more personal for later use.

The next part of the exercise is to bring in secondary research. Let us say that you have drawn an interesting braid detail from a costume in a painting. Complete the sketch with more detail, maybe adding some shadows and a bit of color. Then look for secondary images that are similar visually—in this case, anything with a braided effect or feel (hair, leather, twisted twine, rope, etc.). Using this visual research, try to replicate the braiding yourself with yarn, leather, or even paper. Insert the best and most interesting details in your sketchbook, and archive the rest for future reference. From just one sketch you now have material that can inspire you to take your research a step further.

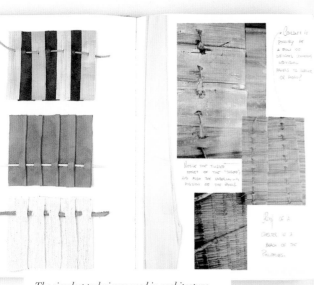

*The simplest techniques used in architecture can provide new solutions to footwear. Here Diego Oliveira Reis has reinterpreted in leather and textiles the slotted and bound building techniques he found.*

*Using a ringbound sketchbook will give a little more space for three-dimensional exploration, as in this "basket weave" experiment by Diego Oliveira Reis.*

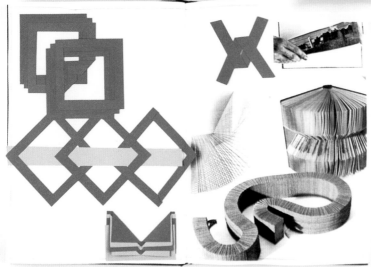

*With paper you can experiment how material behaves both when flat and on a three-dimensional surface, as seen here in Chau Har Lee's research.*

# MOOD BOARD

The mood board is a visual summary of your research. It is the ultimate representation of your ideas that sets the mood for your collection. It acts as the opening page and helps the viewer understand your direction. You can also use the mood board to further inspire your collection's development. Initially it can offer a framework for your design direction, acting as a reminder of the research you have done. It is also a good tool when explaining your collection to an audience, a client, or a design team. The mood board could be as simple as a single image, as long as it accurately sums up your collection.

Mood boards can vary in size anywhere from 8½ x 11 in. to around 30 x 45 in. for a presentation to a large audience. The standard size for presenting a mood board in a college environment is 8½ x 11 in. or 11 x 17 in., depending on the general presentation, so 11 x 17 in. was chosen in this exercise.

## COMPILING A MOOD BOARD

**1.** Review your visuals and select images that relate to your theme.

**2.** Select images that have some of the colors you have focused on during your research.

**3.** Filter these images down until you have five to ten that stand out.

**4.** You can either scan the images, import them into Photoshop, and compose an 11 x 17 in. document (or whatever your preferred size), or select an 11 x 17 in. piece of card or foam board and attach your researched raw materials directly to it. You may wish to mix the two techniques (digital and raw) for a particularly effective result.

**5.** Use your layout skills to make a visually well-balanced document. Do not add unnecessary borders, appliqué, or things to make the board "pretty."

**6.** If you have created the document in Photoshop, print and glue the 11 x 17 in. sheet to either card or foam board.

**7.** Let the images speak for themselves. Do not explain in writing the purpose of each item on the board. It is better to let viewers make their own visual connections.

**8.** The mood board can incorporate some color and material references. If printing color swatches, it is a good idea to attach actual swatches as a reference as well, since color is never as clear printed as it is in the actual swatch. However, it is generally better to keep color and materials on their own (that is, the mood board should be separate from the color/materials board) so that there is not too much information thrown at the viewer at once.

The mood board will be a window to your collection; at one glance it should set the mood for what is to come—as in this example by Michala Allen.

# DIGITAL RESEARCH

Digitization is now ingrained in our society, as more and more of us favor working on a computer and in the digital environment. The ease and convenience of software is highly tempting, and many of us have taken enthusiastically to this way of working. The emotions that are evoked by a hand-drawn line are hard to imitate and it is also much quicker to draw and sketch by hand, but there are interesting new opportunities in the digital realm that could serve as a starting point for something new in the real world. There are cultures that exist only in the digital environment, such as Second Life, and a number of universities have even created digital campuses. Some designers, such as Bart Hess, take the concept even further and design materials that only exist digitally. There is also much discussion about the digitization of color, and whether color looks better on the printed page or backlit on a computer screen. Whichever way we look at it, the digitization of society is happening rapidly and we need to adjust to it. The beauty of this type of work is that there are no physical limitations to a design. As much value as there is in hand-drawing, there is also value in digital work. What we should do is take the best of both worlds and create something beautiful.

## CREATING AN IMAGE BANK

The two types of digital ideas worth archiving are, first, your own images (from your camera—your primary research), and, second, images scanned from existing publications (your secondary research). Both of these can provide strong visual support for further research. If something catches your eye in a newspaper, magazine, or book the quickest way to keep references is to photograph and save, rather than scan—but make sure you use good lighting and take the shots at high resolution. Scanning is necessary if the images are to be used for printed sketchbooks or presentations. There are also digital magazine services, such as www.zinio.com, that offer a great opportunity for researching secondary image material. Remember that all such image copying is allowed only for private use, not for publication, when you would be breaking copyright laws.

The benefit of a digital camera is that you are able to document things easily. It is also very much cheaper than using an analog camera and developing paper images from film. To prevent archiving from becoming unwieldy, there are numerous online image-storing facilities.

## DIGITAL SWATCH LIBRARY

In addition to creating a digital library featuring images of inspirational ideas, you can also create a digital swatch library of materials. It is a good idea to start collecting materials early in your career. When visiting leather or textile shows or fairs, the samples will quickly start to pile up and a digital swatch reference library is an easy way to archive such samples as well as other inspirational materials. There are numerous images of materials available on the Internet, but when you take the pictures yourself you will start to connect with your work from the beginning. The added benefit is that much of the material inspiration will usually be something that you alone have documented. Another great thing about a digital material library is its simplicity. All you need to do is take your camera and take pictures of different surfaces. You can categorize them in your files in whatever way you like: by color, material, pattern, and so on.

Often we become habituated to our environment and do not pay attention to the patterns, colors, and materials that surround us. Try to pay more attention to the ambient stimuli around you. You can get information and inspiration from colors and the different way in which light is reflected from various surfaces. Our surroundings are full of materials, ranging from industrial high-tech metals to beautiful examples of decay: the best "patina" appears when a surface has been worn down by the weather or daily wear and tear—a weathered outside wall, peeled-off wallpaper, a worn leather bicycle seat, and so on. You can also find such inspiration in nature: photographing numerous varieties of plants close up will give you an incredible insight—there are so many shades of green alone. Just make sure to record only the surfaces in your swatch book and not the actual object. We want to focus on the way the material appears and separate it from the actual object, so once you have downloaded the image on to your computer, crop it to focus on the texture or surface. If you want to focus on color, there are even smartphone applications that are able to convert a photographed color into a Pantone code.

You can use the information in numerous ways, for example to create texture to enhance your drawings when working digitally. You can also print these references and use them in your sketchbook. This collection of primary research can be extended to graphics and print design. Of course, the idea of this library is to reference historical or industrial details as a source of information and inspiration alone. Never use other designers' designs directly in your work.

**In brief**
1. Take images of various surfaces using a digital camera, or scan materials.
2. Download them on to your computer.
3. Crop the surface and add it to the library.
4. Categorize the images based on materials (rubbery, decayed, metallic, etc.).

In this digital swatch book the materials
photographed come from domestic
items (furniture) and outside walls.
These swatches can later be used to help
illustrate surfaces on the computer.

# CREATING AN IDEAS BOOK

A personal ideas book is a good place to gather material for future reference. As a creative thinker and a designer you are faced daily with new and interesting ideas from newspapers, magazines, TV, books, museums, galleries, the street—almost everywhere you look. As you might not always want to carry a camera, an ideas book is the ideal place to record what you see. But it is not to be confused with a sketchbook. The ideas book is used to help gather information for future projects. A sketchbook is something you create to record a specific collection or theme.

Find a small book—one that you can easily carry around in a pocket or your bag—and learn to record ideas in the form of words, quick doodles, or more refined sketches. You can even include swatches of materials you find interesting or any other items you come across that can be stuck into the book. The ideas book does not need to be systematic or detailed. It can just have simple line drawings, perhaps a silhouette that you saw in a costume history gallery. It can also hold notes from your daily life. Someone with an interesting hair braiding, for example, might later spark an idea for footwear.

Drawing by hand is still the quickest and best way to do it— it does not require much more than paper and a simple drawing instrument, such as a pencil. As you write down a piece of information, or do a quick sketch, you will automatically learn more from the subject. This is because you will not only have a visual memory of it (as with a digital camera), but also a physical memory imprinted via your handwriting or drawing. Learning to channel your ideas to paper using a pen or pencil will also help you later during your creative process. The ideas book will show you that your life experience can actually provide material for your research. You should be constantly absorbing what goes on around you in the environment.

Notes written by hand will also prove useful. It is important to be able to explain your design process verbally as well as visually, and key words may emerge from your ideas book to help with branding and communicating your collections. An ideas book can be a very powerful tool on many levels.

Once the ideas book starts to fill up, you can start another one. In no time you have built a strong library of personal notebooks, research diaries of sorts that (along with your sketchbooks) will provide a strong archived personal research library, which will serve you through your design career.

## Tips for creating an ideas book

- Find a small, pocket-size book that you can carry with you.
- Make sure the paper is still substantial enough not to bleed through if you use ink to write or draw with instead of pencil.
- Plain white or cream paper always works best, but sometimes it is good to break the routine by using colored or lined paper.
- There are really no rules, logic, or system. The book is just a tool for gathering information.
- Draw ideas quickly and fill in details later from your memory or imagination.
- Write down ideas, names, moods—create personal stories around these concepts.
- Once you have finished one notebook get another one; gradually you will build up an invaluable library of references.

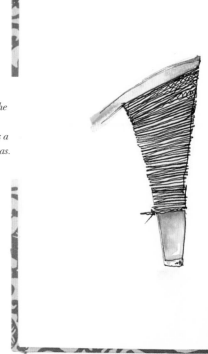

*A good idea can come at any time from your surroundings. The inspirational braided hairstyle, as seen in this instance, provides a starting point for decorative ideas.*

Ideas books can almost become like small sketchbooks with various pieces of inspiration attached to them.

Sometimes using colored paper can be interesting for drawing, not only to break the monotony of white paper but also to provide a new background for your work.

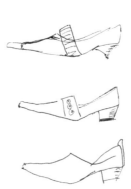

Ideas books come in handy to work on ideas when sitting on public transportation. You can always refer back to those sketches or notes once back in a working environment.

# COLOR AND MATERIALS

Color research is one of the most important—and one of the most overlooked—fields of study in fashion accessories. In the commercial footwear environment color is always one of the top items on the agenda. Companies are interested in trends and consumer behavior, and they want to know how this translates to color. The color direction in footwear is very closely tied into direction and trends in leather. Linea Pelle in Bologna, Italy (see p. 78), is the main materials show where most footwear designers view new directions and trends in leather.

Our view and interpretation of color also varies greatly. For example, the color red can mean so many things depending on whom you ask. But before delving deeper into color, let us review some color theory basics.

Primary colors: red, yellow, and blue. These colors cannot be mixed from others.

Secondary colors: mixed primary colors—green (yellow + blue), orange (red + yellow), and purple (blue + red).

Tertiary colors: yellow-green, yellow-orange, red-purple, red-orange, blue-green, blue-purple, mixed from primary and secondary colors.

A given color has three qualities: hue, intensity, and value. *Hue*: the identity of the color (i.e. red, yellow, green, blue, purple, etc.).

*Intensity*: also described as colorfulness, chroma, or saturation of the color (e.g. intense or dull).

*Value*: also known as lightness (i.e. from black to white).

You can play with color and do coloring tests on paper or in Photoshop to further your color investigation. Unfortunately, footwear color has always fallen into two basic categories: black and brown. This is strictly based on commercial reality, these being the two colors that sell the most. Women's summer footwear is one of the exceptions to the rule. It is not often, even with sneakers, that you see brightly colored footwear for men. Seasonal color selection is used in footwear, just as in fashion. The two main seasons are Spring/Summer (SS) and Fall/Winter (FW).

When choosing colors it is important to understand how color works. Color reacts differently in relation to area covered, appearing lighter if there is more of it and darker if less. This is very important to consider in shoe design. If you look at a large leather skin and cut out a smaller strap for a shoe, the strap will appear darker than the original color of the skin selected. It can easily "disappear" and not create the intended effect.

"Cool" colors, such as blue, seem to recede, whereas "hot" colors, such as red, seem to stand out and jump at you. Areas of hot color in shoes, therefore, draw the eye and can be used to highlight a certain part of the shoe. If you want to focus attention on the heel then creating it in a bright red would achieve this (see p.13 for historical use of red heels). Colors also interact with other colors in various ways, although as shoes are relatively small in surface area the interaction between colors is not always very noticeable.

Having a solid foundation based on color is essential, especially when researching materials. Also be sure to connect your colors to your research and theme. For example, if your theme is something historical and romantic it would not make sense to have color and material references that are futuristic and synthetic. If researching color for yourself or a client, it is equally important to know what you have based your selection upon, and why some color combinations might work better than others. It will make your collection stronger when all parts of the process are connected.

To help you communicate about color with others working in the industry, internationally recognized color-matching systems based on codes are used, such as Pantone. Using such systems is essential, especially when communicating digitally. You might have a swatch and a beautifully illustrated shoe, but a scan of this viewed on another person's computer could look totally different. Coded systems allow you to be certain that everyone involved is talking about the identical color. Color-matching systems for paper and textiles are very sophisticated, but are not so easy to use in leather. It is difficult to match a color from a different type of material or color reference to leather because of its organic nature, the different types of leather, and the impact of various tanning and coloring systems; the type of grain and finish greatly changes the look and feel of a piece of leather, even if the same dye is used.

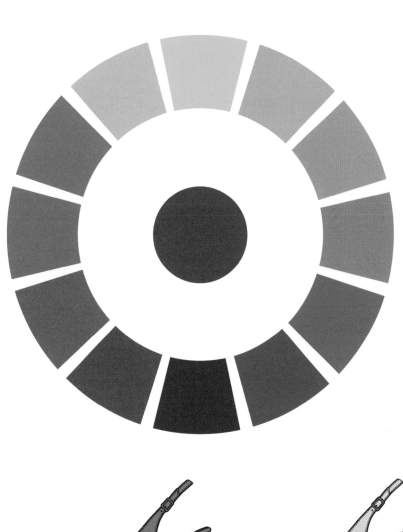

A classic color wheel is based on three primary colors (red, yellow, blue), three secondary colors (green, orange, purple), and six tertiary variations to create a 12-color wheel—the basic system for color relationships.

Color interacts differently depending on its placement. Below, the heel and heel cap of each shoe is the same color in each of the nine drawings, but sometimes appears slightly different because of the adjoining color of the body of the shoe.

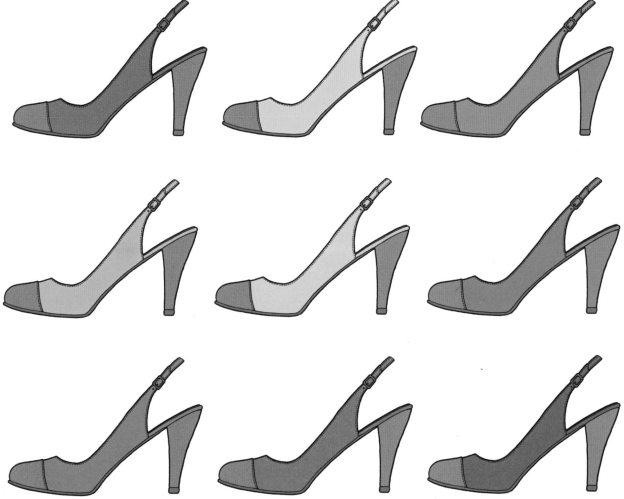

## COLOR AND MATERIALS BOARD

A color board shows the color and materials direction based on your research. It should sit well with your theme and tie into the season. Ideally you would have a separate materials board and color board: the color board would show a clear selection of color used for your collection, while the materials board would link your materials to your colors. The materials board can also be used to demonstrate different treatments that are central to your theme: perforated leather versus heavily grained leather, perhaps. The color and materials boards can, however, be combined.

When creating a collection, one of the most commonly asked questions is, "How many colors should there be in a collection?" The answer is that it can be anywhere from 8 to 15 colors, depending on the size of the collection and on your research. The color and materials board will serve as a point of reference for you and your audience. You do not need to source the exact materials you would use for the collection, but try to find materials that are a close representation of your color story. For example, if you want to use exotic leather, such as python, and do not have access to it, find a good quality image of the material and print it. It is also easy to find interesting materials and references from a number of sources (fabric sellers, hardware and paint stores, and online resellers).

The main point of the color board for shoe design is really to show the approximation of color, the direction you would consider when researching materials for the collection. Of course the more precise you can be the better, but ultimately the exact selection of materials will be made when the collection is being realized. Since color-matching systems, as discussed above, are designed mainly for the print, paint, interiors, or textile industries, it is better to source the actual material and send a sample when needed.

You would also use these colors and materials boards to source the appropriate materials for your collection. The best places to source leather swatches and materials are industry raw-material trade shows such as Linea Pelle in Bologna, Italy (see p. 189). This show is the main materials fair where most footwear designers view new directions and trends in leather. Linea Pelle takes place twice a year, in spring and fall, and is the one-stop shop for the leather industry. Each fair showcases materials a year ahead (so that at the fall show you will find leathers in advance of the following year's fall collections).

In the marketplace some shoe companies have a very systematic way of dealing with color, breaking down the main color story into three selection categories—primary, secondary, and highlights (or "pop"). This is usually the practice for larger companies (such as mid-market and sportswear companies) that have to produce large sample collections for specific markets. In this type of industry the primary color selection will cover the main body of the shoe, secondary will be used on smaller areas, and highlights or "pop" colors will function as accent colors on areas such as laces, pull tabs, or even heel caps. Of course the whole shoe could be just a single color. Other companies follow trend books and create their own color stories based on the directions found in these books.

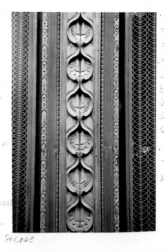

It is good to compile swatches to observe how not only colors but also surfaces react with one another. This was helpful for Diego Oliveira Reis when creating color options for his collection.

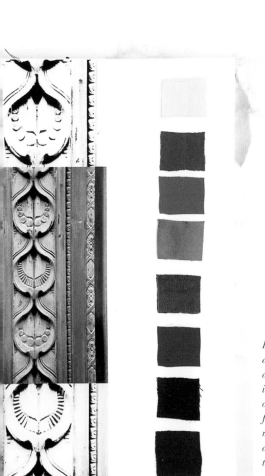

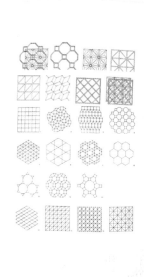

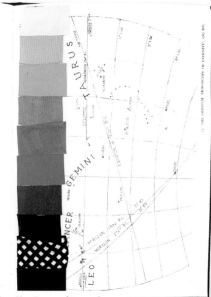

In Diego Oliveira Reis's research, architectural ornamentation and decorations provide endless inspiration for color and textural opportunities to be used in footwear. Try finding matching materials, not only leather but also textiles, in order to bring life to the board.

Chau Har Lee combines color swatch presentation with her architectural and structural drawing base, creating an effective board.

## COMPOSING A COLOR BOARD

**1.** Choose one or two images from your research that show most of the colors that you would like to use in your collection.

**2.** Import the images into Photoshop.

**3.** Select your range of colors (about ten) based on your research and chosen images.

**4.** Under your images in your Photoshop document, create a series of small sample squares or rectangles to represent swatches of color selected from the images. You can specify the colors either using the naked eye or select the color from the images using the eyedropper tool and swatch palette in Photoshop (or the filter menu to pixellate the image and further refine your selection).

**5.** Name the colors. Here you can be creative—yellow might be sun, gold, or banana, for example. Even better, use names that relate to your theme.

**6.** Print the page and glue it either to card or foam board.

## COMPOSING A MATERIALS BOARD

**1.** The materials board should show textures and other surface references that would not display well on a flat color board. Using the color palette from your color board as a base for your materials board, print a Pantone-coded sheet of your palette on 11 x 17 in.

**2.** Find materials that are closest to your colors. If you do not have access to real materials you can use a material that is similar to get your point across (a papery finished leather could be replaced by lightly wrinkled paper). The Internet and hardware, fabric, craft, and thrift stores are great places for finding excellent material references.

**3.** Using double-sided tape, attach the materials to the Pantone-coded sheet in a coherent way, showing how they link to the color palette.

*Chau Har Lee's shoe swatches are not only in leather; this book showcases the various materials used to make footwear.*

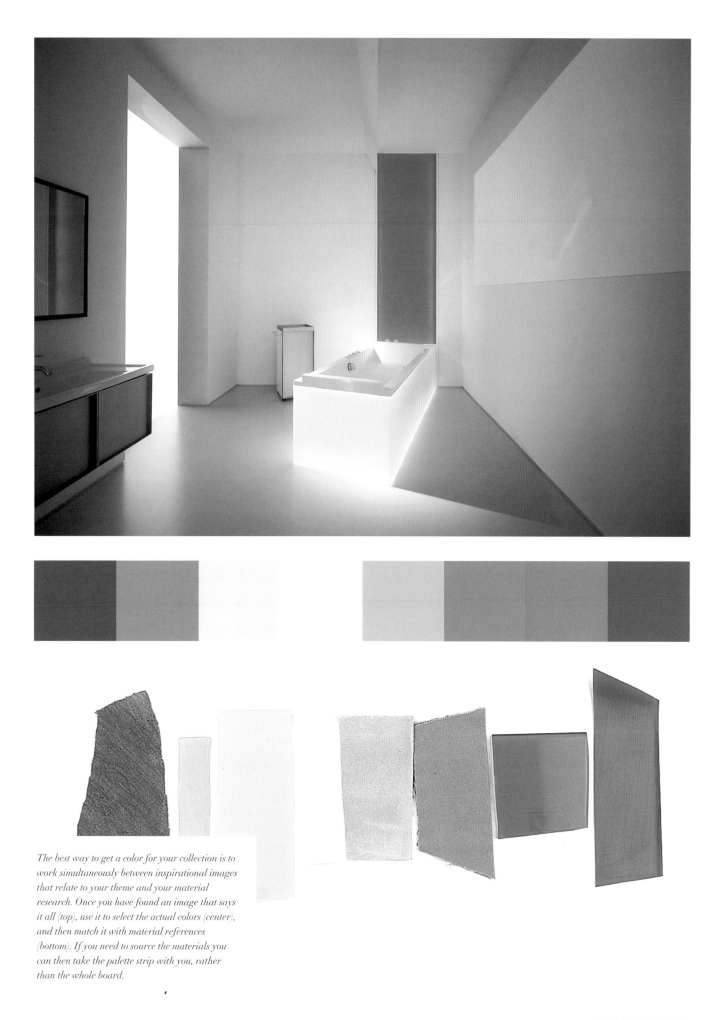

The best way to get a color for your collection is to work simultaneously between inspirational images that relate to your theme and your material research. Once you have found an image that says it all (top), use it to select the actual colors (center), and then match it with material references (bottom). If you need to source the materials you can then take the palette strip with you, rather than the whole board.

# TREND ANALYSIS AND FORECASTING

Trend forecasting is one of the most lucrative areas of the fashion industry, and also plays a role in footwear. For many companies knowledge of forthcoming trends is key, since it is important to stay ahead in a competitive marketplace. Moreover, shoes are among the most profitable parts of many labels, meaning that their parent companies have a vested interested in footwear trends. There are numerous trend agencies that dissect and analyze world trends and consumer behavior. Trend and color forecasting go hand in hand, and are often handled by the same team in a trend agency or a footwear company.

The two basic aspects of trend research are: catwalk trends (what will be in the stores next season) and trend forecasting (what might be in the stores in two or three seasons' time). Catwalk trends are important for the average consumer and for footwear designers working in the fast-fashion category. Fast-fashion brands monitor the catwalk and can have a product in the stores within weeks of a show. Footwear brands, however, need over 12 weeks to produce styles due to the production capabilities. The transportation distance will also have an effect on how fast the product can be shipped to store. This is why footwear is not quite in the fast-fashion category. Trend forecasting focuses more on the cultural direction of the seasons beyond the next one. For a commercial footwear designer it is helpful to know what the trend directions are, in order to gain that competitive edge in the marketplace.

Most footwear designers aim to become trendsetters, showing their designs on the catwalk and creating designs to inspire others, but if you are working for a client it is important to follow the catwalk and global trends. Agencies such as WGSN and Li Edelkoort's Trend Union put out general trend statements, which help companies to design products that have a coherent, unifying story that also makes fashion sense. It is almost as if these agencies do the research for you, and all you have to do is take it to a product. Some agencies, such as Ytrends, specialize in footwear trends, reporting specifically on the world of shoes. There are also leather and materials trend reports, including Material Preview, which are very closely linked to the leather and shoe industry. Most fashion websites that cover the catwalks also cover the accessories and shoe markets.

As a designer you may be working as a trendsetter or a trend follower. If you are a designer in your own right, it is paramount that you should follow your research and, in a way, become a trendsetter. But if you are working with a company or brand that takes cues from upcoming trends (a trend follower), it is then important to know how to translate trend information into shoes.

Some of the footwear-specific areas a forecaster would be looking at as a basis for projections and analysis include:

1. Heel height: What is/are the most frequently occurring heel height(s) this season?
2. Toe shape: Are shoes blunt, square, pointy, or asymmetrical, for example?
3. Materials: What are the key materials? Patent? Exotic skins? Antiqued?
4. Hardware: What type of buckles and other metal components are being used?
5. Color: What are the key colors?
6. Type of footwear: Is the general mood classic or sporty, for example?

What do you do with all this information? As a forecaster you would analyze it and base your footwear-specific reporting on this data. As mentioned earlier, if working with a commercial agency or mass-market brand what you can do with all the trend information is to mix it with your own research, and use the combined information as a source of inspiration for your designs. You could create your own mood board based on your ideas, enhancing it with color information from trend forecasting, maybe completing the general color palette with some of your own selections. It is vital to understand that trend information should be used only to enhance your own work. The problem with many design groups is that they subscribe to trend information and then just copy the information over to their collections, which leads to a market saturated with almost identical styles offered by different brands.

There is no precise way to predict the direction in which fashion will go. Footwear directions, however, do not change as aggressively and quickly as does fashion in general. This is largely due to the fact that most companies do not want to change their last shapes every season, because the cost of this development is quite high. Many companies carry over up to half of their previous season's last shapes, giving them new looks by updating the materials and patterns.

Footwear trends on catwalks are easy to spot, and a key reference for the mass market (especially for fast-fashion companies). Erdem (far left) and John Galliano (near left) both went for the climbing boot inspiration in the same season.

Trend forecasting in footwear often makes connections between other fields of design to show a general direction. Trendsetting designers are often featured, as demonstrated here by Kei Kagami's shoes and Jonas Hakaniemi's chaise longue.

# CASE STUDY: NICOLINE VAN ENTER

Nicoline Van Enter is the world's leading footwear trend forecaster. Her company Ytrends, founded in 2000, provides trend information to many shoe companies, including K-Swiss and Timberland. Van Enter began her career by working on numerous Dutch footwear industry magazines, covering trade shows and brands. She quickly noticed, particularly in the sneaker sector, that there was rapid growth—and she also noticed the way in which footwear was more and more linked to seasonal trends. Van Enter realized that there was a gap in the market: several companies reported on apparel and textile trends, but there was no company that specialized in footwear.

Besides having a degree in graphic design and considerable experience in the footwear sector, Van Enter feels that public speaking played an important role in her career development. "Lecturing is what made me—being able to go in front of an audience and deliver a trend vision has been the most important tool of my trade." Teaching the client how to apply trends to a product is what Van Enter and her company specialize in. She does not want her audience merely to listen to her suggestions, but also to learn how to apply the information themselves.

### Q How/where do you start with the new season trends?

**A** There is no fixed starting point for the research; that is continual and largely intuitive. I travel a lot to cities around the globe, visiting trade shows and exhibitions of all kinds—not just footwear—taking pictures and talking to people. I also collect articles, images, and videos from newspapers, magazines, books, and websites that somehow strike a chord in me and I save those on my computer all the time. Initially I just put all new stuff in one huge folder, without sorting it.

The market dictates when it needs information—like a document and/or a lecture—to kick off a season. Usually that is about 18–24 months in advance of that season. About a month or two before the release date of my new seasonal trends I start sorting my info, taking into account whether I am going to present Summer or Winter. The reason why I don't sort my info while collecting is that I like to keep an open mind and have my info lead me in unexpected directions.

First I print thumbnails of all files and lay them out on a huge table, making different groups and discussing those with various people in my team, to avoid any kind of bias or tunnel vision as much as possible. Then I start seeing meaningful connections and fully realize why I was drawn to certain things during my research. It is my aim to go beyond the look of a certain trend and identify the developments in society that cause this trend to occur. So I connect style and aesthetics to social, technological, ecological, and financial developments. Once I have defined the most influential long-term developments I create my trend themes based on those, rather than on mere color or material.

**Q How has the world of trends changed in the last few years (if it has)?**

**A** There have been a lot of changes but the rise of the Internet has been the most influential, shifting the focus from printed trend books to digital, multimedia information. Furthermore, it makes it seem as though much more information has become readily available, yet this has also raised the question as to what trend information really is. To me it is not just a bunch of photos of what is "cool" right now: this kind of info can cause "design panic" and makes it more difficult for companies to develop and maintain their own style. The task of a trend forecaster in the fashion and design industry is to analyze what is available now, both in terms of style and technology, and then translate that into a future vision, giving a clear opinion on where things are moving and why, actively helping companies to make wise long-term decisions for product development. I think we should all realize that this is something that has not changed because of the Internet, it has just become more important in order to make sense of the "information overload."

**Q What is the most important part of your forecasting?**

**A** There are two equally important parts to my forecasting: the Ytrends publications that I release each season, which are digital and interactive; and my tailor-made consulting. The publications give my own vision of future footwear trends from a broad perspective and are also the base for the lectures that I give all over the world. For those companies that hire me as a consultant, I translate my themes into ideas that are particularly directional for them. Often, though, advising customers which trends to stay away from, because they do not suit their brand, is even more important than telling them which trends are relevant.

**Q What is the most pleasurable part of forecasting?**

**A** To me the pleasure of forecasting is that it is such a broad business, which combines super-creative "blue-sky thinking" with very down-to-earth and practical advice. For footwear it is especially exciting, because this is both a fashionable and a technological product.

**Q What advice can you give a footwear design student who is interested in your field?**

**A** Please remember that forecasting is not just about what, but also about why! So if you feel you can identify trends, make sure you can also clarify why each trend occurs. To explain that background properly you need to have the skills to express yourself in both images and words. Being able to give lectures and to explain your vision in conversations with a client is something that is often neglected in programs that aim to educate fashion forecasters, yet these verbal skills are absolutely essential. Obviously it also helps if you speak several languages, both for communication and for research, and computer skills can help you visualize your ideas in a convincing way.

*The Ytrends blog offers a wealth of information both to the footwear industry and shoe enthusiasts alike. The content is always graphically engaging and forward thinking.*

# CASE STUDY: NIELS HOLGER WIEN

Niels Holger Wien works as a color and trend forecaster based in Halle, Germany. His job involves a variety of projects but mainly revolves around the world of color and color forecasting. He is currently part of the trend board of the German Fashion Institute, specializing in color trend research (since 2004). Niels has represented the Deutsches Mode Institut (the German fashion body) in Intercolor since 2007. Intercolor is an international platform for color research and development, consisting of an interdisciplinary group of color experts from 13 countries. He also works for the Swiss Textile Organization (since 2009), focusing on color and trend research for the Swiss textile industry.

## Q How did you end up working in the color industry?

A It was a hard choice to make, deciding between languages, music, math, art, and design. I opted for fashion design plus graphics—still called "clothing design" in a very strict Bauhaus manner when I started my studies in 1988 at the renowned Burg Giebichenstein University of Art and Design Halle. Color occurred very naturally in sketching, drawing, making collages, draping, cutting, sewing, knitting, embroidering, photographing—color was always a matter to work with. Color as language, particularly its different use between the sexes, became one underlying theme of my diploma, "A Subjective History of the Androgynous."

After the reunification of Germany in 1990 I wanted to expand my cultural experience, and I gained the chance to study at the Academy of Fine Arts in Antwerp, Belgium. Afterward, my first years of work experience were dedicated to and shaped by the staging of fashion. Styling fashion shoots and staging fashion trends for trade fairs led me to focus on the associative power of colors and textures to create and combine narrative pictures around fashion. The next step in my ongoing learning process was obvious to me: Li Edelkoort's Trend Union in Paris, home of View on Colour, one of the most influential seasonal color trend guides, where I worked first as an intern and then as a freelancer for six months.

## Q What is color?

A Physically defined, color is an effect of light—of the reflection of light. Without light we are not able to perceive any color or to distinguish shades. And of course this is connected to our vision, our ability to detect electromagnetic waves of a particular length.

Color is about seeing and light, about refraction and reflection: color is the perception of the frequency, or wavelength, of light, and can be compared to the way in which pitch (or a musical note) is the perception of the frequency, or wavelength, of sound.

Three things are needed to see color: a light source, a detector (e.g. the eye), and a sample to view. Our color vision is

*Niels Holger Wien in his job as color and trend forecaster researches the effect of color on every aspect of design.*

nearly unlimited: a trained, highly sensitized eye is able to distinguish up to three million color shades. In comparison, the Pantone color system—one prominent color communication tool for the fashion and design industry—specifies only about two thousand colors.

Beyond all physical definitions, color has developed into a very sophisticated language to symbolize concrete things as well as to express feelings and emotions—and to connect these material and intellectual fields.

The emerging of color expression is integrated into the human evolutionary learning process and is closely connected to the evolution of language and speech. For instance, to convey information regarding an edible plant, leaf, or berry our ancestors at some point needed an abstract expression to complement and refine the description of form, surface, handle, smell, taste, and so on. In human history expressions for certain colors did not occur until they were needed for the purposes of communication, or when those colors could be reproduced.

**Q Is color important in the communication of ideas?**
**A** Color is a medium by which rational thoughts and unconscious feelings are interconnected, and in this sense it is a means of communication. Sight (visual sense) is considered to be the dominant of our five senses. Visual information is the primary, fastest, and easiest way to send impulses to our brain—though of course it works in conjunction with the other senses.

Color can symbolize objects, materials, actions: think of traffic lights, the sky, a sunset; imagine a cherry, warm lips, fresh water; recall forget-me-nots, a favorite painting, Kermit the Frog. When a certain color shade has established a memorable link (whether consciously or unconsciously) to something we know, it can become an abstract symbol for it—in the same way that the letter A of the alphabet has become a symbol for the sound (phoneme) A.

In this abstract way color has been used as a means of distinguishing groups of people following certain religious, political, cultural, economic, and other ideas or beliefs or theories. Historical, cultural, ethical, and of course individual contexts are essential to understand and to decode those color links. To communicate using colors it is indispensable to have a close connection to the zeitgeist.

**Q What is your opinion on color education in design schools?**
**A** Color is closely linked to material and surface, so in that way it is an integral part of every design process— I personally understand color as matter. Material is defining, in the way it influences color and the impact of color. Having enough time for experience is often a problem during a study course: basic studies in drawing, painting, molding, typography, art and cultural history, and so on require an

# CASE STUDY: NIELS HOLGER WIEN

intense period, which is often shortened and limited. As color is considered to be already part of those basics it is mostly underestimated as a matter for study in itself.

Learning color should be regarded as learning a foreign language—and the more languages we speak the more we interlink them, find parallels and derivations. Learning color language should enhance sensitivity to cultural links and differences and, as with any new language, it should encourage open-mindedness.

**Q What is the best way to learn about color?**
**A** Color perception is a very individual process, linked to individual experiences and sensory skills—therefore I see no best way but only individual ways of learning about color.

However, as color is a visual experience it is helpful to train the visual sense. The more one works with color material the better one can distinguish shades. Collecting colored material samples creates a personal archive and reference tool. It is useful to get a notion of color and its material surface, for instance the different shading of shiny and matte finishes.

As color and light interact it is striking to discover how color impression changes with different light: light and shadow, changing time of day, changing season, changing region—all influenced by the altitude of the sun. Becoming aware of the light temperature of artificial light sources helps in understanding color variations.

As nature provides unlimited color shades try to catch them—as the American photographer Robert Weingarten did in his "6:30 AM" series, when he photographed the horizon every day at the same time from the same position. No one image is the same as another.

Colors interact with one another, and it can be suprising to experience how a single shade changes when exposed to other colors and shades. Different levels of contrast or harmony may boost or soothe juxtaposed colors. To create color summaries of pictures, paintings, or photographs is a good way to analyze color interaction. Remember Photoshop's pixel and mosaic filters and try to create such color abstraction of images manually.

If color is communication, try to consider it as a language with a special vocabulary, grammar, and poetry of its own. Just as learning vocabulary helps to refine one's expression, so inventing as many as possible expressions for one color family brings color vision to a point. Think of the Inuit culture's proverbial thousand synonyms for "snow" and "white."

**Q How does color link to other senses?**
**A** With color as a medium of light and visual perception, it already captures the most prominent place among our five main senses. But none of our senses operates separately. The most

common link exists between our sense of smell (olfaction) and our sense of taste (gustation), when in the interplay with olfactory stimuli our taste is expanded beyond the basics of bitter, sweet, sour, and salty to more complex flavors.

In expressing our perceptions we often use cross-sensory metaphors—that is, illustrating one sensory impression by other experiences, such as "screaming red" or "sweet pink." Such metaphors are driven by individual experiences or culturally perceived patterns. Color perception has cross-sensory potential. Linking it to other senses is part of the learning process of color language.

### Q Where do color trends come from?

**A** Nowadays color trends are one aspect of the way in which the production of modern consumer goods is linked with the evolution of the zeitgeist. Color trends are a fundamental part of complex trend research—important for a community model based on economic growth and ever-increasing production. But color trends can be detected throughout human cultural history, although they were not labeled as such—and they did not have such a seasonal impact as we have experienced in the past few decades. Reviewing cultural eras, one can detect prominent and leading color harmonies that have been connected to the manual and/or industrial discoveries and achievements of their respective times.

Maybe our desire for change dates back in evolution and is a part of the human condition. Our ancestors had to roam in order to satisfy the basic needs of life, while we are relatively bound to urban settings. We are creatures of habit, we cultivate our likes and dislikes. New things catch our attention, they stimulate our curiosity. We like to touch, to eat, to listen, to get, to wear, to share. We get used to our finds; they may become favorite pieces. They become companions—until they become time-worn and start to bore us. This makes us desire something new, unfamiliar, untamed. A circle is about to restart. Everyone can discover those habits in his or her life, but these circles (or waves) of curiosity, liking, habituation, and boredom are like individual fingerprints and have different amplitudes.

Fortunately it is not easy to synchronize these feelings and the feeling for color remains very personal.

*These boards by Niels Holger Wien are meant to challenge imprinted memories— to make you stop and think… what does lime green really mean?*

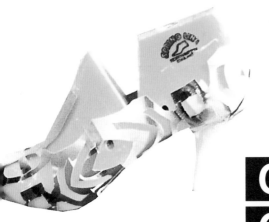

# CHAPTER 4
# COLLECTION
# DESIGN

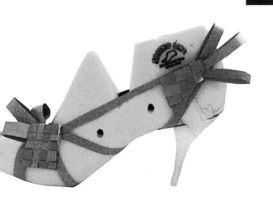

**The collection will be the ultimate result of your research. It should be a carefully composed group of footwear that tells an interesting story. But how do you translate the research into a range of shoes? In this chapter we will look at quick and effective ways to take the researched material and develop it into the designs that will be the seeds of your range. We will also look at collection theory, examining the basic requirements for building a strong and harmonious collection.**

# DESIGN DEVELOPMENT

In the design development stage you begin working with ideas from your primary and secondary research. This is the time to start taking your ideas and thinking, "How can I bring this material to my shoe collection?" The point of development is to bring references from your collected material to your drawings, and from there into your designs. Again, it is not about how "a table leg"—makes a good heel... but rather how that table leg can mutate into various options that consequently point the way to new opportunities. Design development does not have to be systematic, but can be free-flowing, dissecting concepts or expanding them into designs. This enables you to push your ideas as far as possible. In this section we will look at how to stretch your creative imagination using a few quick exercises.

All the exercises use a flat side view because this is the easiest to draw. To increase the difficulty level, do the same exercise with a three-quarter view, back view, etc. This will give you more practice at drawing three-dimensionally.

Any of these designs can be used in your sketchbook as reference material. Either copy or cut them out and paste them into your sketchbook where appropriate.

Helen Furber offers different options
for her collection development, using
the same parameters but applying her
lines in different ways.

## EXERCISE 1: DEVELOPMENT SHEETS—EVOLUTION OF QUICK IDEAS

This exercise is designed to help you take a reference (such as a table leg) and distill it creatively into various options for footwear. Sometimes it is difficult to know what to do with an inspirational item, and how to introduce it into the collection. This system will help you to overcome that initial dilemma and quickly draw out basic ideas. You can then expand these ideas further in your collection. It is important not to spend too much time at each stage of the exercise. You can draw inspiration from any visuals or material samples for this exercise.

**MATERIALS:**

Pen; 8½ x 11 in. paper; 11 x 17 in. layout paper; primary or secondary research images; marker pen.

**TIME:**

Spend ten minutes maximum per sheet; quick ideas are better.

**STEP 1**

Take a piece of paper, about 8½ x 11 in., turned horizontally (landscape), and draw the outline of a last that you will use in your collection.

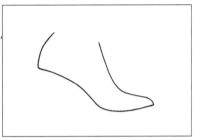

**STEP 2**

Trace the shape six times on to 11 x 17 in. layout paper.

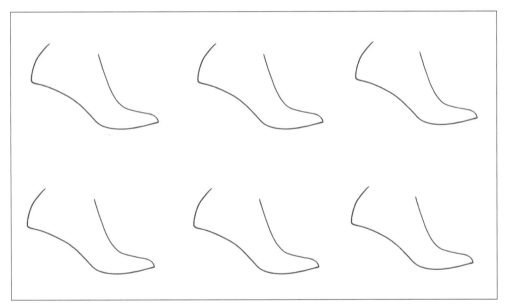

**STEP 3**

Study one of your inspirational images from your primary or secondary research.

**STEP 4**

Starting with this image, draw exactly what you see on top of the first of the last shapes. Try not to fit it into the shape, just draw it on top. Copy as much detail as you can. Make sure to draw with a quick, free hand to get the best results.

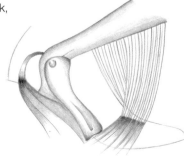

## STEP 5

Put your image away now. Taking inspiration only from your first drawing, move on to the second last shape on your 11 x 17 in. sheet. Make the drawn image a little more shoelike so that it "fits" this second last shape a little better.

## STEP 6

The third, fourth, fifth, and sixth drawings will be variations of these. The final drawing should bear hardly any relation to the first.

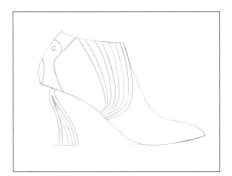

## STEP 7

Finally, spend some time adding a little definition to the drawings—use shading to bring out your shoe designs, and markers for shadows. Repeat this process five more times (five sheets, each with a different inspirational image) to create a total of 36 initial designs.

At the end of this exercise, lay out all your drawings in front of you. Make a note of five or so of your favorites and thus you have the seed for your collection. From this you can move on and develop your concept further and further. The idea is not to take an image and think straight away

that it would look good as an item on a shoe. Occasionally it can work out that way, but generally you should be drawing such conclusions only at the end of the exercise.

## EXERCISE 2: ISOLATION—NOT LOOKING AT THE BIGGER PICTURE

Sometimes you see something but are not really sure how to take inspiration from it. Perhaps the image does not necessarily directly relate to your research, but a detail within it does. This exercise (or pair of exercises) will help you isolate these details from the bigger picture. It will help you connect, focus, and start creating your own world of inspiration.

**MATERIALS:**

Black 8½ x 11 in. card; 5 x 8 in. paper; scissors or knife; pencil; 11 x 17 in. layout paper.

**TIME:**

Spend ten minutes maximum per sheet; quick ideas are better.

### 2A) SHAPE ISOLATION

**STEP 1**

Take a piece of 5 x 8 in. paper, turned horizontally (landscape), and draw the outline of a last shape that you want to use in your collection.

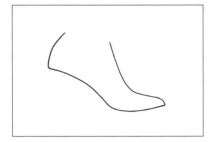

*Isolation also works on self-created surfaces, as seen in this example by Diego Oliveira Reis.*

**STEP 2**

Trace the shape six times on to 11 x 17 in. layout paper.

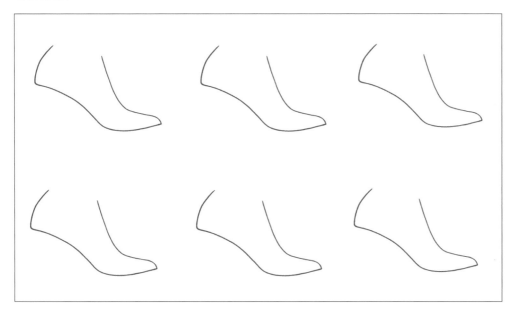

## STEP 3

Cut a circular or triangular hole into the
card and place the shape on a selected
image, over the part you want to develop.

## STEP 4

Copy the area in detail over the first last shape.

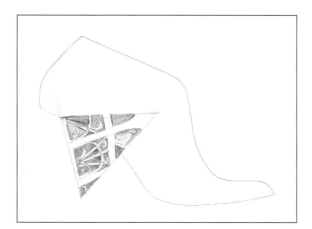

## STEP 5

Develop the detail further, and take ideas from it to
develop the rest of the last shapes.

## 2B) SHOE SHAPE ISOLATION:

This part of the exercise is especially useful when developing surface ideas such as print and patterns.

### STEP 1

Take a piece of 8½ x 11 in. paper, turned horizontally (landscape), and draw the outline of a last shape that you want to use in your collection.

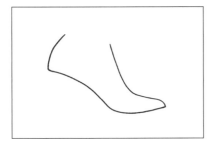

**Tip**
You can also use the isolated form to get inspiration from fabrics and materials. Place the shape on top of different surfaces such as leather, knit, or other woven materials. Take pictures or scan these shapes to create interesting material presentations.

### STEP 2

Trace the shape six times on to 11 x 17 in. layout paper.

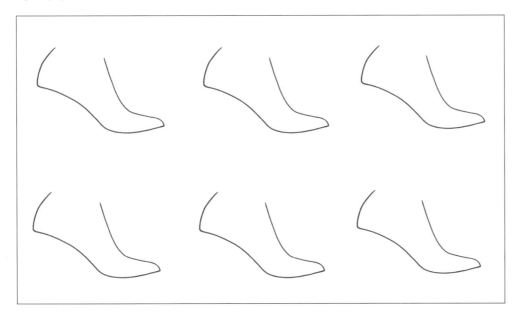

## STEP 3

Cut a last or a shoe shape in the card and place the shape on a selected image, over the part you want to develop.

## STEP 4

Copy the shoe-shaped area on to the first of the last/shoe shapes on the 11 x 17 in. paper.

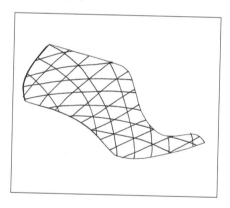

## STEP 5

Develop your ideas further in the same way as in the previous exercises, looking at what relates best to your research.

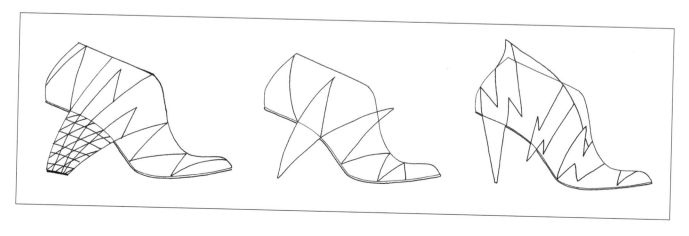

Draping is interesting and fun, and can spark great ideas for your collection. It helps you get away from the two-dimensional mindset of drawing. Becoming familiar with a last and having the three-dimensional object in your hand will give you a better idea of how your design can work on the foot. It can inspire new shapes and silhouettes, and help you develop ways to better translate your thoughts into an actual shoe. Draping is commonly practiced in fashion design, when material is manipulated directly on a dummy to create a design. This system works equally well with footwear and the shoe last. You can drape your last with literally almost anything you have to hand: wire, a pair of pantyhose, paper, even cookie dough. Ideally, use materials that are close to your theme. If your research relates to nature, for example, use materials found in your local park, your garden, or the countryside, such as leaves and bark.

**Tip**

Any serious aspiring shoe designer should buy a last. These can be ordered from last-makers. Check with your local shoe industry representative to find local producers. The Internet is also a good source. Another excellent resource for locating manufacturers is the international Linea Pelle trade show in Bologna. Their website lists the exhibitors that sell shoe-related materials.

*Draping will bring new life to your design, as demonstrated here by Diego Oliveira Reis. Simply by using paper you can explore the space around the foot.*

Once drapes are photographed, bring them into your sketchbook in order to cross-reference your inspiration and material references, while creating a captivating and inspiring spread. This is Diego Oliveira Reis's work.

This draping by Jin Hong was done using various materials. When draping, take pictures from various directions to get a feel for the object's three-dimensionality.

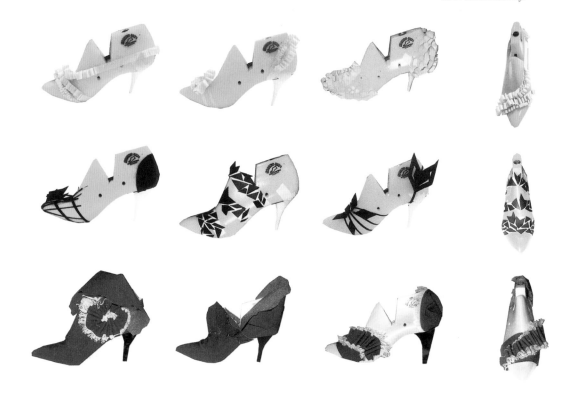

## MATERIALS:

Last; masking tape; draping material (can be anything); 8½ x 11 in. paper; 11 x 17 in. layout paper.

## TIME:

In the drawing section spend ten minutes maximum per sheet; quick ideas are better.

## STEP 1

Prop up a last and drape it with material of your choice. Take a photograph.

## STEP 2

Repeat step 1 another eight times. Position the nine pictures in a grid using a computer software program, three to a row.

## STEP 3

Take a piece of 8½ x 11 in. paper, turned horizontally (landscape), and draw the outline of a last shape that you want to use in your collection.

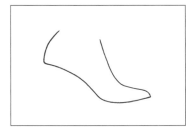

## STEP 4

Trace it six times on to 11 x 17 in. layout paper.

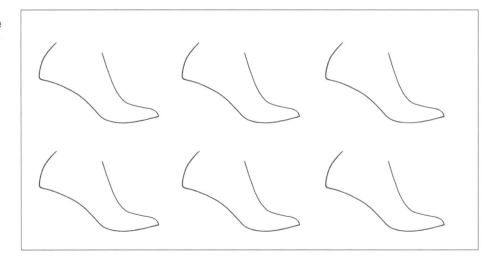

## STEP 5

Choose a draped last to work with.

## STEP 6

Starting with this image, draw exactly what you see on top of the first last shape. Copy as much detail as you can. Make sure to draw with a quick, free hand to get the best results.

## STEP 7

Put your image away and, taking inspiration only from your first drawing, move on to the second shape on your 11 x 17 in. sheet. Make the drawn image a little more shoelike.

## STEP 8

The third, fourth, fifth, and sixth drawings will be variations of these. The sixth drawing should bear hardly any relation to the first.

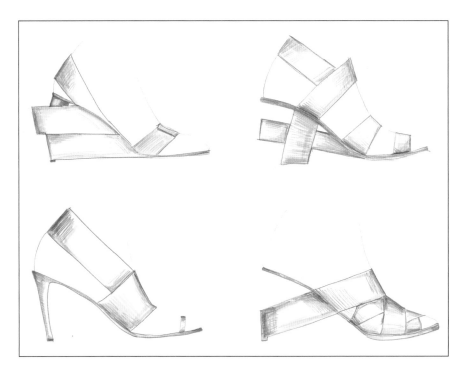

## EXERCISE 4: SILHOUETTE AND VOLUME

One of the biggest limitations of footwear design is the shape of the human foot and the limited functionality of it. Footwear design is not only about the surface of the shoe but also about the silhouette and what can happen in the area that surrounds the foot. Many contemporary shoe designers have already started to question the basic shape of the shoe, bringing us new dimensions and shapes.

The draping exercise is a perfect platform from which to develop shape ideas, since the outlines provide new silhouettes naturally. If you take one of the draped items from the previous exercise, for example, and draw an outline of it, you might find a completely different silhouette that will enable you to create new shapes and take your designs to an altogether new dimension.

*Shoe design often forgets the space that surrounds the foot. This is not the case with Kei Kagami's shoes; they explore the areas that are usually overlooked, creating interesting new ways to look at footwear.*

*Georgina Taylor's shoe nests inside a leather shell, creating a captivating combination and a new form and silhouette for the foot.*

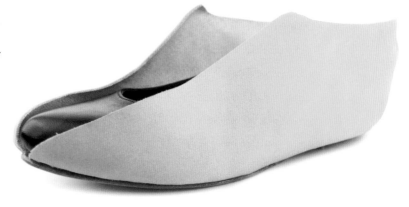

## MATERIALS:

Images of draped shoes; pen; layout paper or computer software.

## TIME:

Spend ten minutes maximum per sheet; quick ideas are better.

Looking at the traced area, start to develop new ideas based on the shape. Take the silhouette and extend it so as to create new shoe shapes. You could also try turning the new silhouette upside down or flipping it from left to right in order to give it new life.

## STEP 1

Either trace a photograph of one of your draped shoes or use computer software to re-create the silhouette of one of them.

## STEP 3

Let your creativity take over and start creating new designs by incorporating ideas from your research, and then developing these ideas further.

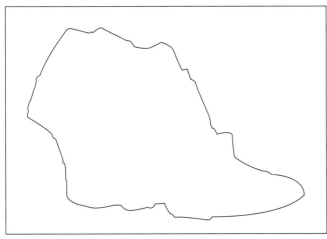

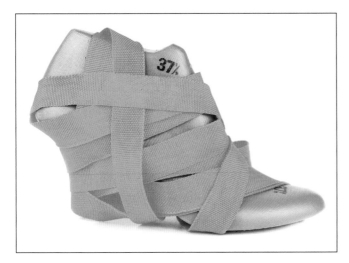

## EXERCISE 5: COLLAGE

This method is very creative and lots of fun. Sometimes absurd combinations of images can give interesting results and help with the creative process. This exercise is also designed to get you started with the development process. You can take images from your research and juxtapose them, creating something new but recognizable. You can then take these collages, scan them, and work on developing further ideas for your collection.

### MATERIALS:

Images from your research or magazines; scissors; glue or tape; drawing paper; pen or pencil.

### STEP 1

Choose visuals that relate to your theme (but not shoes). Use body, textural, architectural, and mechanical references and cutouts to create a shoe collage.

### STEP 2

Redraw the collage with pen or pencil.

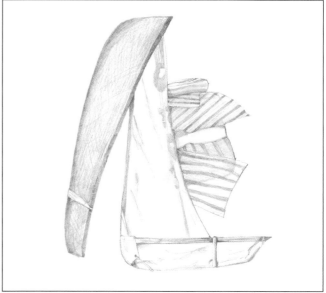

Draw further versions and develop the designs into realistic
pieces of footwear. Try also other perspectives.

## EXERCISE 6: 2-D–3-D

It is sometimes difficult to understand fully how a two-dimensional drawing will work as a three-dimensional shoe. This is why it is important for any aspiring shoe designer to make a pair of shoes by hand at least once, in order to gain a complete understanding of the process. If this option is not open to you, one way to approximate the process is to try to make a 3-D model of your design, preferably on a last. As we have seen, you can draw almost anything you like, but taking that idea and applying it to a last is another matter altogether. The following exercise will help you to become more familiar with the three-dimensional nature of the foot.

### MATERIALS:
Last; masking tape; paper; marker; scissors.

### STEP 1
Choose a design from your drawn collection.

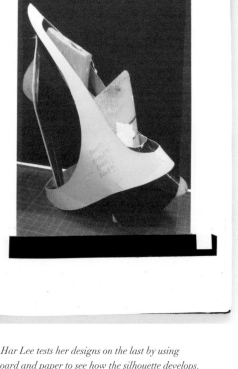

*Chau Har Lee tests her designs on the last by using cardboard and paper to see how the silhouette develops. By looking at the 3-D model, she can then see whether the design needs further modification.*

**Taping a last**

There are numerous ways to cover a last with masking tape. For this exercise we are creat a surface on which you can draw. The easies way is to start from the tip of the last and work your way back. Keep flattening the tape with your fingers to keep the surface even. sides and the back of the last can most eas be taped by using vertically placed pieces tape. Finally, cut the excess ends to creat neat drawing surface.

### STEP 2
Tape a last using masking tape. There are many different ways to tape a last, but for this exercise do it simply to provide a surface to draw on.

## STEP 3

Draw your design directly on to the tape-covered last.

## STEP 4

Complete your design with paper elements that you apply to the last as well. For example, if you drew a sandal strap, cut the shape of that strap out of paper and stick it on to the last.

## STEP 5

Go back to your original drawing and see if there is anything that you would modify after the three-dimensional exercise. One of your ideas might not work in three dimensions, or you might suddenly find a new way of solving a problem once you can see the design on the last. For example, in your flat drawing a strap placement might look great, but once it is drawn on a taped last or stuck on as a paper strap, the placement might not look right and you might decide to change the angle.

**TIP**
Many fashion schools offer short courses in shoemaking at different levels. See p. 176.

# COLLECTION THEORY

After the design development you can start building ideas for a collection. There are two main stages: last design and collection design. At the start of the process the most frequently asked question is, "How many pieces should a collection have?" In fact, the more pressing question is actually, "How many lasts should a collection have?" The most expensive part of the sample development process is the last and bottom development (the latter being an outsole and insole combined), which is the basis of your design. Development and manufacture of the last, bottom, heel, and first upper is a time-consuming process requiring specialist skills. To put all the components together and fit them correctly is also labor-intensive and very costly. It therefore makes economic sense to limit the number of times you need to do this and thus the number of models developed each season. Even large shoe companies use a limited number of bases and then build collections around them. A seemingly wide range of shoe styles can be achieved by simply modifying heel shapes and varying the materials. If you look closely at designers' collections you will see that there might be numerous different styles but the underlying basic shape and heel heights are limited.

A first collection for women could include a flat-, mid-, and high-heel last. If you design two flats, four mid-heel styles, and three high-heel styles you will end up with nine styles. Then if you make each style in two color versions you will have 18 pieces to show as a debut collection. You might use the same shapes for the following season, perhaps adding a couple of new shapes, thus developing a comprehensive collection to show. Showing 20–30 pieces per season is an acceptable average.

For men's styles it is basically the same. With men the collection usually revolves around playing with styles rather than heel heights. You can base your collection on three lasts initially and then slowly add new last shapes and styles.

But what is the essence of a collection? The most important aspect is that the collection should have your handwriting. Essentially, what would make someone buy your collection as opposed to that of the designer next to you? They should be drawn to your individual style. The best way to achieve this is to use your design development as a foundation for building your collection. Additionally, a collection should "make sense": since collections are shown for either Spring/Summer or Fall/Winter, it makes no sense to do a fur-lined knee-high boot, a flip-flop, and a sport shoe all together. It is also important to have a strong personal design identity, especially when showing the collection for the first time. The collection should be exciting enough to get your audience interested in your product, yet at the same time concise enough not to overwhelm with too many choices. Anyone should be able to scan your collection and think "I get it."

*Georgina Taylor ties her collection together by shape and material, while making each shoe interesting enough to stand on its own.*

*Rae Jones's debut collection uses
materials and details, such as
a natural color lining, to keep
the collection together. The boot
adds interest on a different level,
yet is part of the same family.*

The last is a key element of a collection's development. There are two main parameters that need to be considered in last design: the toe shape and the measured heel height of the last (without a platform addition). Of course, when you add a platform at the front of the shoe the heel height is increased. If you change either one of these (toe shape or last heel height) your shoe becomes another model; if you add a platform it does not become another last but will still be another "style." This is important to remember when designing the collection because if you stick to a limited number of heel heights and toe shapes it will make the collection more concise.

## Shape

The shape of the shoe is dictated by the shape of the last. What shape do you want your shoes to be—blunt, pointed, square…? Another part of the shape design to consider is the toe spring. The toe part of the shoe can be raised upward from the ground or can be almost flat to the ground. Because of the rocking motion of walking there is always a need for some toe spring, but it can be very high for stylistic reasons if desired.

On paper anything is possible, but when developing a shoe that has to function it is important to work closely with a professional who can turn your designs into reality.

When submitting your ideas to your last-maker it is important to send a clear drawing of the shape you have in mind. Ideally you should visit the last-maker in person to discuss the shape you need. Sometimes it is difficult to get things right the first time, especially if you are only communicating long-distance via e-mail. Generally, when visiting a last-maker you will be shown previously made lasts that are close to your design; using these as a basis you will then discuss the changes you want in order to make your individual version.

## Heel height

Heel height is what determines the "pitch" of the last, or the "last heel height." The heel height is usually measured by taking a perpendicular line from the back bottom level of the last straight up to the back of the heel. When material such as a platform is added under the ball of the last it will naturally increase the height of the heel, but not the pitch of the last.

Heel height is one of the key factors in footwear design. The identity of the shoe in relation to the heel height is set by comfort levels but also by social mores. High heels are generally considered sexy, and flat heels more utilitarian. In this respect, you need to consider what is the general mood of your collection. Is it about evening elegance, avant-garde fashion, comfort, or a mixture of directions? Do you want flat or mid-height heels or do you want to focus on high? Flat can be a totally flat last (such as sneakers), but an average flat shoe will usually have a ½–1 in. heel. The mid-heel (1–2½ in.) is usually the bestselling height for women, probably because of the combination of comfort and height. Since flat heels have a certain image, as do high heels, if you can design mid-height heels that are interesting and above all sexy you will have a highly saleable product on your hands. High heels are generally considered to be anything above 2⅜ in. With platform additions heel heights are almost limitless.

With men's styles the heel heights are around the standard half inch or so, although there are some men's labels that no longer limit themselves to standard men's heel heights.

*Exaggerated toe spring created by a long last shape does not affect comfort, but does give a particular look to the final shoe.*

*The heel height on this Stuart Weitzman shoe is increased by a double platform. This does not need a new last, since the actual heel pitch is not changed. The same last can be used for a lower-heeled shoe without the double platform.*

This shoe by Chau Har Lee,
shown alongside its last,
demonstrates how the last shape
will bulk up after materials
such as a toe box and lining are
added on top of it.

Now that you have designed (and possibly already sourced) the "heart" of the shoe—the last—you can start designing styles using your last as a base, beginning to explore ideas for heel shapes and uppers. Here we have broken down which parts of the shoe can and should be designed.

*Try to find a unifying look for the collection. Shape is the main focus of Raffaello Scardigli's "stealth" collection (below left, below, and opposite), based on the idea of anonymity.*

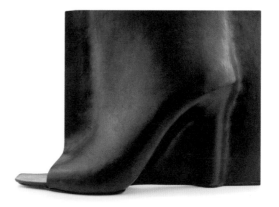

### Heel

The heel's shape is very important to consider within the overall design. It can signal and reflect your theme, and influences the overall balance of the shoe. The heel can be made to your specifications (though this can be costly) or you can source a heel that is close to your design. A heel can make a very strong statement. Often designers employ a very aggressive heel, leaving the rest of the shoe very simple in order to balance out the overall harmony of the shoe.

There are numerous new material mixes that you can use to create heels that reflect your theme. With advances in heel technology the shapes can be developed into fantastic creations, from slim towering stilettos to Plexiglas wedges. Do make sure, however, that the shoe you are designing is not just about the heel and its variations.

*The heel can bring the collection together through shape or material, as seen here in Georgina Taylor's full metal heel.*

*In this shoe, Julia Lundsten's label FINSK focuses on a heel shape that brings a whole new dimension to the silhouette.*

*Chau Har Lee's gold heel nicely connects the upper part of the shoe, creating a continuum between the two parts.*

*Try to find a unifying look for*

## Upper

This is where you can use your creativity to its maximum. The upper part of the shoe is the most visible part. The pattern options and color and material combinations are endless. Anything can be created, from the simplest sandals to the most extravagant boots, and everything in between. One good way to make sure that all the elements of your collection sit well together is to repeat a certain line in the pattern pieces of the shoe, perhaps keeping the counter line (the part that covers the back of the heel) the same across the collection. Or you could have a similar style of pattern cuts in the shoes, keeping all the patterns rounded or sharp, in keeping with the theme. The choice of a raw edge or a folded edge will send a totally different message about your shoe and the craftsmanship—folded edges are more time-consuming and bring a more elegant finish to the final product, while a raw edge would give perhaps a more craft-referenced finish.

*The upper is the area that is most visible; it allows you to be the most creative by using various techniques and materials.*

*Stitching and the ways in which edges are folded can make a big difference to the final look of a shoe. Raw edges (bottom) will give the shoe a less refined feel than folded edges (top).*

## Stitching

It is worth paying attention to the smaller details. You can use stitching as a design element, for example adding stitch lines to create shapes on the surface of the shoe. The thickness and color of thread can make a big difference to the look of the shoe. Depending on the country, different manufacturers have different ways to code stitching width, but at the design stage it is enough to show whether the stitches should be thick or thin. Usually stitching is done "tone on tone," but with color-contrast stitching you can bring interesting effects to the shoes.

## Lining

It is also important to consider the lining at the design stage. The lining can be designed by adding perforations or other references that relate to your design, but generally designers tend to keep it simple and work with colored linings.

## Sock lining

This is the first thing you see when looking inside the shoe, and is generally where branding is placed. Your logo needs to be carefully considered, to ensure it works well not only on a letterhead but also inside a shoe. There is not much space in the middle of the sock lining, so it is important to design something that can be read easily and clearly; very thin lines can be problematic with stamping, for example. Other options for branding, such as fabric labels, are available. The edge of the sock lining can also be designed—cut with a zigzag or a more rounded style, mixed with brogue-like perforations, and so on. Keeping the edge the same across the collection can work well as a brand identifier: this is commonly used in women's sandals, where the inside of the shoe is exposed.

## Hardware and ornaments

Hardware—such as buckles and closing mechanisms—can be designed and made to your specifications. Most designers, however, source existing items from a manufacturer, since the making can be costly. There are, again, endless options for closures but it is always important to consider the finishing and how it relates to your theme. If you have a historically referenced collection, a futuristic buckle or a plastic sporty zipper pull would probably not work well.

*The thickness of the stitches will make a big difference to the look of a shoe. Thicker stitches convey weight and rawness.*

*Small things, such as the flat edge trim on this shoe, can be used to unify a collection. The finish and shine on buckles have to be specified as well.*

*The sock lining is visually one of the most important parts in the shoe; Rae Jones is the first thing you would see when you put these shoes on. So color, logo placement, and material need to be carefully considered.*

*Hardware can also act as a place for branding, as has been done here with the metal zipper pull on one of Julia Lundsten's FINSK shoes.*

## Outsole

Usually the sole is made from leather, rubber, or man-made materials, such as ethylene vinyl acetate (EVA) or thermoplastic polyurethane (TPU). You can also find soles made from crêpe and wood. Soles are either cut to size (from a larger piece of sole material), or bought ready-made to fit your design/last. Sole design is an important part of the overall design. You can easily add design elements to leather outsoles using embossing techniques and coloring techniques. More complicated man-made soles can be developed as part of your design, but the molds can be very expensive (and this cost will multiply as the molds need to be made in each shoe size).

*Michala Allen's sole is decorated by using flocking, bridging the heel and the bottom of the shoe nicely.*

*Rubber-and-hemp mixture molded shoe.*

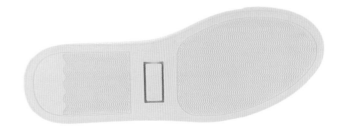

*Molded rubber outsole.*

*PVC (thermoplastic polymer) molded outsole that imitates a leather finish.*

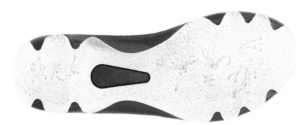

*TR (a rubberlike material used in soles) with embossed molded designs.*

*Aku Bäckström uses fruit-crate material in this shoe, which is made using numerous unusual materials and finishes.*

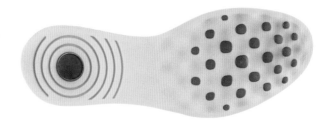

*Layered TPU (thermoplastic polyurethane) molded outside that brings dimension to the sole.*

*Balls of plastic as they look before being melted down to be used for soles.*

*This material is a rubber and cork compound; it will be used to create rubber soles with cork pieces for texture.*

## Materials

The material used for the uppers of shoes can vary greatly. Leather is generally the best option, though is by no means the only choice. The leather can be designed to your own specification, but most of the time you would source the material to match the color and texture you wish to use. Some leathers are more suitable for clothing and accessories than shoes—ask the tannery or the leather retailer (in the material research stage) if the material is suitable for footwear. There are ways to add your own designs to leather, such as embroidery and laser cutting (as seen in the nappa examples below—nappa is a leather that is ideal for manipulation due to the softness and durability of the skin). Finishing sprays can also greatly alter the shoe's appearance by creating, say, a matte or shiny surface finish, and can even be used to add special effects such as applied seams. There are many processes that tanneries use when designing leather. The most common surface treatment in materials is color. The second is changing the surface appearance with such techniques as perforations, cuts, pleats, and embossing, to name just a few.

There is a wide diversity of non-leather upper materials. Shoes can be made from many types of materials—textiles, imitation leathers, plastics, rubber, even straw and cork. The upper material can really be almost any material, as long as it can be somehow attached to the bottom part of the shoe, and is durable enough to stand walking and the manufacturing process. Materials that are not suitable for uppers include textiles that are not treated and backed with more durable material: these can crack, and the color may bleed when wet.

*These leather swatches show that leather can be treated many different ways, and combined with other materials.*

*Nappa with laser-cut motifs on organza backing.*

*Laser-burned designs on nappa.*

*Laser-cut motifs on nappa sheepskin with organza backing.*

*Laser-cut motifs on nappa sheepskin leather with organza backing.*

*Embossed sheepskin nappa leather.*

*Printed nappa goatskin with machine embroidery.*

*Laser-cut holes provide a channel for the machine to stitch motifs into this sheepskin nappa.*

*Pleated and hand-colored sheepskin nappa.*

*Sheepskin nappa decorated with overstitched elastic bands.*

*Laser-cut designs on nappa stitched on rabbit fur.*

*Benjamin John Hall's collection shows an interesting mix of materials and colors not often seen in men's footwear.*

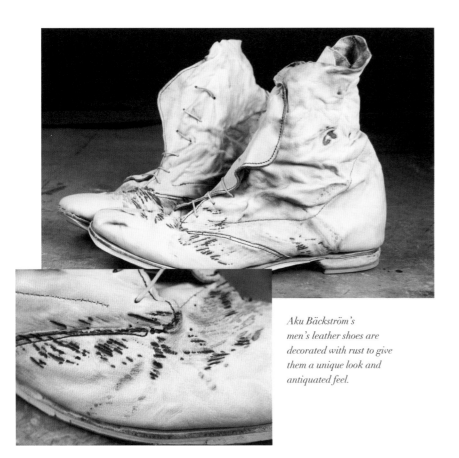

*Aku Bäckström's men's leather shoes are decorated with rust to give them a unique look and antiquated feel.*

*Noritaka Tatehana's platforms are made using embossed leather; they show how embossing has a more profound effect on a larger surface.*

## PUTTING IT ALL TOGETHER

The best way to start a collection is by reviewing your research. Think about your theme and your initial shoe design ideas. Also, you should think about the message you want to send with your collection—is it to be experimental, commercial, or elegant? Your research should naturally point you in the right direction. Don't forget that everything is possible on paper. Pushing forward-thinking ideas is recommended, and innovation is needed. The concept in design is most important. Just make sure that in your research you can support your idea, and sell your concept to the viewer. Be careful, however, not to make your collection too thematic. Research should not be taken literally—this can sometimes result in a collection that is too referenced. The viewer should be able to discover the theme from your collection, rather than look at it and see direct references all at once. This is why design development is so important. Another critical thing to remember is that shape and silhouette are what adds value to your design. Anyone can do surface treatment or add print and color to a shoe. Ultimately what you need is a well-balanced mix of interesting materials and new forms and silhouettes.

*Helen Furber's footwear, shown right and below in different environments, shows how the mood of a piece can change depending on the background against which it is shown.*

*In Chau Har Lee's collection each shoe tells a story but they also work well together as collection; shoes should work equally well in both environments.*

Start thinking of your lineup and how many last shapes and heel heights you will have. As mentioned earlier, three or four shapes are usually suggested in debut collections (see p. 110). A good way to select pieces that will form your collection is to choose from among the designs that emerged from the various creative development exercises discussed earlier (see pp. 94–109). Choose your favorite 20 or more initial designs (with varying shapes and heel heights) and start developing the designs further. Take these ideas and then narrow them down to 10 or 15 ideas you would like to use as a base for your collection. The next thing to do is start analyzing the toe shapes and the heel heights. If there are pieces that you like but are not the right height or shape, simply make corrections in order to use them on the last shapes you have chosen.

A collection might include a concept shoe or a show piece. This piece will be the attention-grabbing item of the group while the rest can follow safer routes. However, it is crucial to have something that keeps your collection together. The lasts naturally tie the models together, but it is also a good idea to keep such elements as buckle styles or seams similar. There really is no rule on how to do this. Look at the overall harmony of the collection and decide if you want to focus on anything in particular. If all the items look too similar it can be boring, so to get to a pleasing final result a careful editorial eye is needed. The best way to design is to let it happen naturally. If you design something and it just doesn't feel right to you, regardless of the rules, don't do it! Learn to listen to your inner design voice.

Finally, it is important to put all your complete designs next to one another for a lineup to see the full collection more clearly. You can then start playing with the colors and details that will bring the group closer to a real collection. Stay true to the original ingredients and the theme, and do not be tempted to add items that do not come from your design development. This can ruin the balance and the natural flow of the collection.

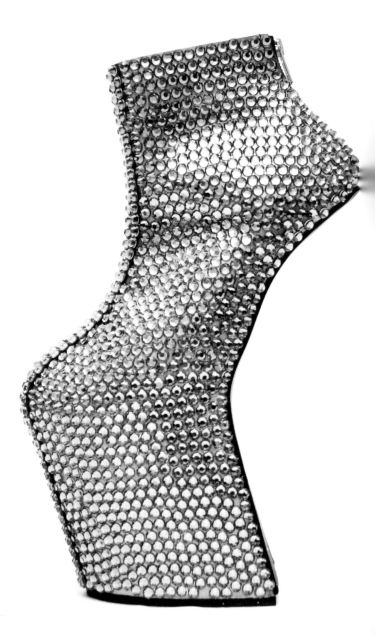

*A shoe collection, just like a fashion collection, can have a show piece that will make a statement — as seen here in Noritaka Tatehana's glistening platform shoe.*

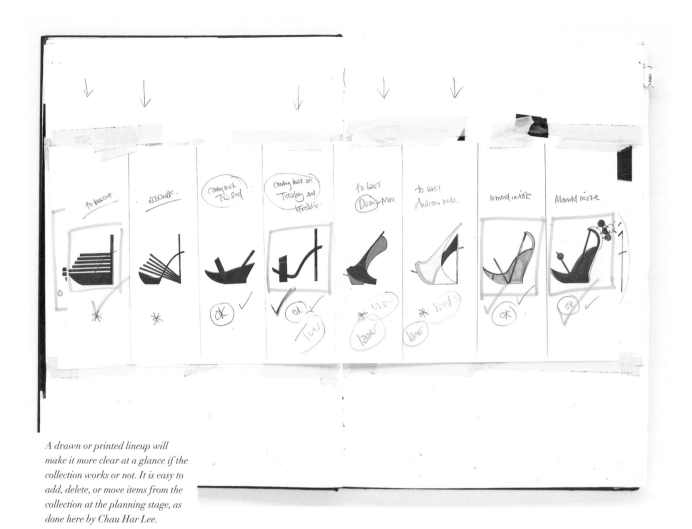

*A drawn or printed lineup will make it more clear at a glance if the collection works or not. It is easy to add, delete, or move items from the collection at the planning stage, as done here by Chau Har Lee.*

**Tip**

In the beginning, a quick way to start finalizing your design is to take a photograph of your propped-up lasts and trace the outlines or use them as a base. This way you can focus on your designs, rather than trying to draw the shapes correctly each time. After some practice you will be able to draw shoes and ideas freehand, and tracing will no longer be needed.

*You can prop your last up with anything if a heel is not available. Just make sure to leave some "toe spring" for a more natural silhouette.*

# CASE STUDY: MINNA PARIKKA

The Finnish shoe designer Minna Parikka studied at De Montfort University in Leicester, UK, where she received her Footwear Design degree in 2002. After graduation she returned to Finland and launched her label, ultimately settling and opening her flagship store in the center of the capital, Helsinki. She produces her collections in Spain and is involved in all aspects of the collection development.

Minna Parikka footwear is designed for confident women by a confident woman. Parikka herself embodies what is perhaps a shoe designer's ultimate dream, with her eponymous label and a boutique that sells her footwear, bags, scarves, and small leather goods. The brand has a strong design identity that carries across all levels of the business, from the products to her boutique and online presence. Every aspect has been considered, carrying through the unifying style that is a mixture of fun and flirty looks.

*Minna Parikka's shoes use strong colors, interesting details, and always have a signature look about them.*

**Q How/where do you start with the collection design?**
**A** I always start to collect ideas when I am at trade shows selling the previous collection. It's inspirational to meet buyers and other designers, and see what works and what doesn't. Airplanes are really good for design work.

**Q When you design a collection do you sometimes/always/never have a theme?**
**A** Usually there is a theme that brings the collection together. It might be a color palette or a certain mood.

**Q How do you research your collection (is there a researched story, materials research, etc.)?**
**A** Materials, colors, and refined details are very important. The component research is done locally in Spain.

**Q How do you gather inspirational ideas? Book? Mood board? Mood or ideas wall?**
**A** I don't gather so much inspiration from pictures and I don't make mood boards. For me it's important to look at fashion, people, design, art, travel… and keep all the memories in my head. When the time for designing comes I draw moods from my head more than look at trends in magazines.

*Hearts are often featured in Minna Parikka's world, from the flagship interiors to shoes such as this one.*

**Q Do you draw the initial ideas in a sketchbook?**
**A** I draw thumbnail sketches on some random pieces of paper. From those I develop bigger line drawings on 8½ x 11 in. sheets.

**Q Do you use computer-aided drawing or only draw by hand?**
**A** I am so traditional that I do everything by hand, using pens, pencils, and black marker pens.

**Q What is the most important part of your design cycle? Theme? Design? Sampling? Production?**

**A** Design is the most important for me as a person, but the manufacturers do the sampling so they need to see my idea correctly. There is no point in designing something perfect if the sampling and production people cannot read the detail correctly.

**Q What is the most pleasurable part of the design cycle?**

**A** To see the finished product with all the amendments.

**Q What advice can you give to a budding footwear designer?**

**A** You need to have a lot of patience, passion for shoes—and trust your own vision.

*Minna Parikka in her flagship store in Helsinki, Finland. The whole brand, from her store fittings to the shoe boxes, carries her design identity.*

# CASE STUDY: ROSANNE BERGSMA

Rosanne Bergsma studied Product Design at ArtEZ Institute of the Arts in Arnhem, the Netherlands, graduating in 2009. Within this discipline she chose to specialize in fashion accessories. As a recent graduate she has decided to keep her production in-house (not manufacturing them industrially), while working as a design consultant. Her women's footwear has a very modern approach, with a focus on shape references from objects and architecture.

**Q Why shoes?**
**A** I feel at home in creating a shoe design. From the inspiration to the sewing machine, I love to challenge the laws of the shoemaking process and create innovative shoe designs.

**Q How/where do you start with the collection design?**
**A** I seek inspiration in construction methods. This is the beginning of a collection. In my work the inspiration usually becomes an abstract reference; it doesn't necessarily have to be discernible in the final design. I'm truly pleased when this approach results in a new "image."

**Q When you design a collection do you sometimes/always/never have a theme?**
**A** The theme is the construction, and shapes that arise from it. I always start with making tests derived from a detail or a feature of the inspiration. Then I try to extend them to a shoe through adding them on the last. The designs for the shoes originate through molding on the last: I drape the material around a last. I explore to what extent the manner in which my source of inspiration is constructed could result in a new approach to the designing of the shape of a shoe. After molding I make a pattern. I do not draw. I have much more feeling for the final form by molding. I know immediately what is possible and what isn't. With drawings I always stay in the familiar image of a shoe. Draping gives me a lot of freedom.

**Q Do you draw the initial ideas in a sketchbook or only take pictures of your drapes?**
**A** Sometimes I draw the different designs of a collection on a piece of paper for an overview of the collection, but most of the time I take pictures of my drapes. I don't draw to design.

**Q How do you research your collection (is there a researched story, materials research, etc.)?**
**A** I study the construction. The research consists of how I can realize my inspiration in a shoe design. My work revolves around new technical solutions and the details that come from them. Traditional craftsmanship is central to this approach. This is my route to quality. To me, craftsmanship also stands for luxury and exclusivity. The luxury is in the visible attention and precision with which my designs are made, as well as the choice of the best materials and techniques. This is why I choose to work with leather: it still is the most suitable material for

*Rosanne Bergsma is often inspired by construction, tension, and ideas of suspension. She does not draw, but designs directly on the form by draping.*

the shoes I design. As a result of my passion for the trade, I custom-make the shoes myself.

**Q How do you gather inspirational ideas? Book? Mood board? Mood or ideas wall?**

A In my work it is not about atmosphere. I think that's why I don't gather a whole wall of inspiration. Usually, I just have a few different pictures of a shape.

**Q Since you drape your designs how do you communicate your ideas to a factory, or do you do all your own production?**

A When I communicate with a factory I draw my designs. I design for a couple of commercial shoe brands. I don't have my own shoes in production yet.

**Q What is the most important/pleasurable part of your design cycle? Theme? Design? Sampling? Production?**

A The most important part is certainly the design and seeing when a good design is created.

**Q What advice can you give to a budding footwear designer?**

A Stay yourself and have fun with it!

# CASE STUDY: STUART WEITZMAN

American shoe designer Stuart Weitzman runs the international footwear company of the same name started by his father, Seymour, in the 1950s. Seymour Weitzman inspired young Stuart to design and produce his first shoe at the age of 16—memorialized in bronze, this would mark the start of Stuart's lifelong career in shoe design. Following in his father's footsteps, he went on to develop the factory into one of the most successful footwear companies in the world. Today, Weitzman is involved with most parts of running his company. He is also a trained pattern-cutter; understanding the intricacies of the shoe and the way elements interact is an important part of the design process.

The Stuart Weitzman brand is recognized the world over and is available in more than 45 countries. It is also one of the most featured products on the celebrity circuit. Possibly the most expensive shoe ever to walk a red carpet was a couture piece of his decorated with diamonds that was worn at the 2004 Oscars by the singer Alison Krauss. These shoes were priced at $2,000,000.

The company's shoes have been produced in Spain in the same production area for more than 30 years—a critical factor in achieving a consistently high-quality product season after season. It is also important to have close communication with the factories. According to Weitzman, "It's not unusual for me to spend half of my 100-plus-hour work week overseeing operations in my factories." Overseeing all aspects of production is key for the designer: "My name is on the shoe, I put everything I have into making whatever style it is the best I can possibly make it."

For Weitzman, design is a full-time occupation: "I actually never stop thinking about design—maybe that is why I have over 400 styles in each season's collection." The designs are naturally edited down to a smaller collection that is then selected later for production. The collections are made cohesive through materials and color palette. Weitzman's inspiration comes from numerous sources. He says, "I believe creativity can be sparked by the simplest details. Some forms of past, present, and future inspiration for me have been things I have seen on the sidewalks of New York City or the Spanish countryside, a favorite old movie, or the changes in nature with each season." As with most designers his research is wide-ranging, taking him from fashion to film to history to global street styles. He uses traditional methods and materials in his design process: pencil and paper for sketching and hand-coloring for illustrations.

When asked what the most fun part of the design cycle is, Weitzman answers: "Fit trials—because if it doesn't fit, then the shoe will stay in its box in the closet." And the advice Stuart Weitzman gives to budding future designers is essentially to love what you do. "I view this as my hobby, not my job—so continue to do what you love for a living and it will fill your days with happiness."

*Stuart Weitzman was born into the shoe business. He is a globally recognized designer with several stand-alone stores.*

*Stuart Weitzman has not adopted new technologies but continues to design using traditional "drawing" methods. The end results — left and above — are elegant and sexy.*

*Stuart uses interesting material and surface mixtures, as seen in this pair of shoes that has a chain-covered heel and metallic-finish leather.*

*These Stuart Weitzman sandals have a slight platform and a stud-decorated, partly leather-covered Plexiglass heel.*

# CASE STUDY: PACO GIL

The Paco Gil footwear company is based in the city of Elda in Spain's eastern Alicante province, where Paco Gil himself designs, directs, and coordinates his in-house design team, overseeing all aspects of the design process. The brand has been in existence for more than 25 years and offers elegant, innovative, and sensual footwear to women that, according to Gil, is the "ultimate accessory."

**Q How/where do you start with the collection design?**

**A** Normally, our collections have a continuity with previous seasons. We are aware which styles have been the most accepted, what kind of last and heels work the best, what textures were liked, and so on. Once we have this information and feedback for the season we start a new collection.

**Q When you design a collection do you always/never/sometimes have a theme?**

**A** There are several fashion and accessories fairs we visit. We interpret the moods and information from them in the light of our own opinions and choose the topics that we consider the most suitable for us and our customers. We do not have one single theme but use several themes in our collections.

**Q How do you research your collection (is there a researched story, material research, etc.)?**

**A** I consider myself a worker in the design world and I try to instill this approach in my team. Think of a building: it always begins with the foundations. Our collections always start with the last and the materials that will create the base on which we build our collections.

**Q How do you gather inspirational ideas? Book? Mood board? Mood or ideas wall?**

**A** Basically, the ideas are formed in our heads until we reach the point where we must begin to develop the collection. Then we write and draw our ideas in a small notebook with sketches and notes on the materials.

**Q Do you draw the initial ideas in a sketchbook?**

**A** We usually draw some initial sketches, but I want to stress that the basis to a shoe collection is lasts, materials, and ornaments.

**Q Do you use computer-aided drawing or only draw by hand?**

**A** Although we have computer design programs, we are from the old school and prefer manual design.

**Q What materials do you prefer (pens, pencils, watercolors; what kind of paper, etc.)?**

**A** Always with pencil and rubber. Sometimes we color the drawings and we use sheets of ordinary paper.

**Q What is the most important part of your design cycle? Theme? Design? Sampling? Production?**

**A** The design process is like a chain. If one link fails, it all fails. All processes have the same importance.

**Q What is the most pleasurable part of the design cycle?**

**A** I love working with wood to make perfect lasts and heels that will become the base of my shoes. I also like to take part in the process of tanning leather, as it is an important process that makes my collection different.

**Q What advice can you give to a budding footwear designer?**

**A** Students must realize that design work is very hard and that you never finish learning.

*In this red wedge sandal Paco Gil captures the essence of his label with its suprising mix of color and material.*

*Paco Gil often plays with color and creates confident shoes for the modern woman.*

# CHAPTER 5
# PRESENTATION

# PRESENTING YOUR IDEAS

**How you present your designs and ideas is important because you want the viewer to understand clearly who you are as a designer. Your audience can vary. However, when presenting your collection to an academic audience, such as for the final presentation at the end of term, the level and the quality of your presentation are as important as they would be if you were showing it to the press or to a potential buyer. In this chapter we will focus on the presentation of your research and final illustrations. There are three basic areas to consider: the overall presentation of your concept, the illustration of the designs and the technical or line drawings, also known as "flats."**

The overall presentation "sells" your collection to the viewer. It can be used to tell the story, or theme, and is a marketing tool, demonstrating your vision. You must consider the complete delivery and the environment for your work, not only the final illustrations. When putting your presentation together you need to think about the whole package—including the types of paper, print and folder used. You can look to your research to find materials to extend your theme and draw your presentation together—since you have done the research, you might as well use it fully.

The illustrative style of your drawings is something that you have to develop yourself, like discovering your own language. Illustrating your collection does not necessarily need to involve only drawing. There are endless ways to illustrate your world, from traditional drawing, through mixed media, to film and digital options. Your illustrations can be a useful visual communication tool with future employers or even with the press.

The technical or line drawings clearly explain your design. These do not need the creativity of the illustration, serving only as technical instruction sheets, accurately showing the design of the shoes.

In this chapter we will cover some basic drawing techniques, and discuss which materials will produce the best results in your presentation.

*Milan Sheen's designs drawn on a model create a human connection and a captivating environment for the shoes.*

*This spread by Milan Sheen has all the elements that explain the shoe. The illustration sets the mood, the flats clearly explain the shoe structure, while swatches of material and color complete the picture.*

Dr. S. Schachenmann

*Sandra-Noella Schachenmann incorporates her self-portrait, presenting a collection based on the idea of identity and cloning. Each shoe (below) is a manipulated clone of the original, covered in a stockinglike material.*

CLON SNSCH 3
cloned by Dr. S. Schachenmann

CLON SNSCH 1
cloned by Dr. S. Schachenmann

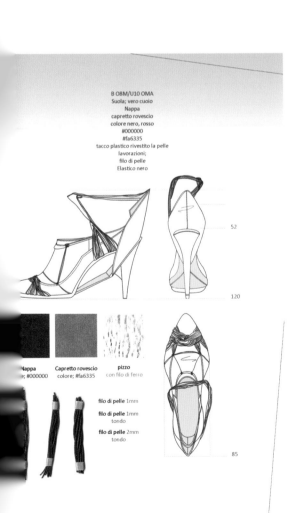

B 08M/U10 OMA
Suola; vero cuoio
Nappa
capretto rovescio
colore nero, rosso
#000000
#fa6335
tacco plastico rivestito la pelle
lavorazioni;
filo di pelle
Elastico nero

52

120

Nappa
e; #000000

Capretto rovescio
colore; #fa6335

pizzo
con filo di ferro

filo di pelle 1mm

filo di pelle 1mm
tondo

filo di pelle 2mm
tondo

85

CLON SNSCH 4
cloned by Dr. S. Schachenmann

# DRAWING

Drawing the feet and footwear can be a daunting task, especially if you are unsure whether your drawings will turn out to be of high enough quality. Here we explore a few simple techniques to help bring some life to your drawings. The point is to communicate to your viewer the mood of the collection and your "hand" (i.e. your personal drawing style). It is important to try as many techniques as possible, in order to find the materials with which you most enjoy working. Some designers like to illustrate their designs through hand-drawing, whereas others may prefer to use other ways to deliver their design ideas, such as using computer programs.

Drawing by hand, however, still plays a very important role in the fashion world. It is the quickest and most effective way to demonstrate your designs. Hand-drawn illustrations can be very seductive and most of the top European fashion houses state that a hand-drawn portfolio is essential. Anyone can draw using computer programs, but hand-drawn illustrations will show your real personality.

Nevertheless, illustration software is widely used in the footwear industry for its clarity and its transferability across different computer platforms. We can safely say, therefore, that it is important to learn both manual and computer-aided illustration. It is not enough to know how to do black-and-white line drawings (whether hand-drawn or computerized): colored drawings are much easier to understand. For example, in a black-and-white drawing it is sometimes difficult to understand which part of the upper is cut through and which is actually a covered section of the shoe.

*Even rendering the flats is sometimes useful, in order to understand what is a cut area of the upper and what is actual material. Here you can see the cut area without color (top), and it is difficult to determine if this area is a space or another material. The middle drawing shows more clearly the upper cut through. The bottom drawing shows the upper not cut through.*

## ESSENTIAL DRAWING MATERIALS

### Paper

*Copier paper* There are various grades of copier paper you can use. As a basic stock paper, the cheap non-glossy copier/printer paper is the best. The non-glossy matte surfaces are ideal for ink line drawings and quick pencil drawings. Use 8½ x 11 in.

*Watercolor paper* There are also different grades of watercolor paper. For our purposes, standard-weight watercolor paper is adequate, and 11 x 17 in. is recommended for size.

*Layout paper* Layout paper is thin paper that is ideal for quick drawing exercises and for tracing. It is not the easiest paper to source. Try to find lightweight 11 x 17 in. paper that is good enough for ink (bleed-through) resistance.

*Sketching paper* Standard-weight sketching paper is available in art supply stores, commonly in sheets of 8½ x 11 in. and 11 x 17 in.

### Pens and pencils

Suggestions are:
• 0.5 mm micron black ink pens;
• A 0.5–0.7 mm mechanical lead pencil;
• Average sketching pencils range from 2B to 4B; use whichever hardness you find easiest to work with.

### Watercolors

Watercolors vary greatly in quality and price. Suggestions are:
• An artist-quality watercolor paint set;
• Watercolor pencils, which are an excellent and more controlled way to add color to your drawing;
• A set of watercolor paintbrushes in various sizes.

### Color markers

Markers are harder to master, but can give an interesting texture to the surface of the drawing. They are used widely in sneaker design. Prismacolor or Copic markers are highly recommended.
• 1 mm tip black marker pen;
• Prismacolor or Copic markers (light gray and very light brown are essential).

## DRAWING THE FOOT AND FOOTWEAR BY HAND

The best way to understand footwear and its dimensionality is to practice drawing feet, then continue with a last, and then finally draw actual shoes. It is necessary to keep practicing to develop your drawing skills. It is impossible to draw exactly what you see because we see in three dimensions, but have to draw on paper in two dimensions. But that is not the point. What you want to do is to draw your impression of what you see. There is no point in trying to copy styles that you cannot draw: just keep drawing what you feel confident about and, most importantly, natural with. You should feel confident about your personal style and nourish it. When drawing:

- Do not constantly look between the item and the paper. Have a good look and then, from memory, draw a sketchy version of the object.
- Do not start drawing from one part of the item and build the drawing up. Most likely your drawing will either end up not fitting the paper, or will be otherwise out of proportion.
- Draw a general overview of the item and then start filling up the image with more details and definition.

The exercises here are designed to help you get some practice in basic footwear drawing. Draw them all without using an eraser to avoid disturbing the flow of the sketching.

*The quickest and best way to put down creative ideas is still by hand. Hand-drawn ideas can then later be developed into computerized drawings.*

*In this age of digital information, hand-drawn shoes can provide a different way to publish work. In these designs by Hiroshi Yoneda, you can see both the illustrations and the final product.*

## EXERCISE 1: THE FOOT

**MATERIALS:** Pencil; paper.

Ask someone to pose for you, since drawing a subject from life is always best. If this is not possible, use photographs of feet taken from different directions. Start with a flat outside view of the foot. Then move to an elevated-heel side view, and so on. This will give you an idea of how proportions work when the foot is in different positions. It will also help you learn how to draw the curving silhouette of the foot, a good starting point for many future drawings. At first you can just draw quick outlines, and then start adding some shadows and details to give depth to your drawing. Try drawing the feet from as many angles as possible in order to get a full understanding of the foot.

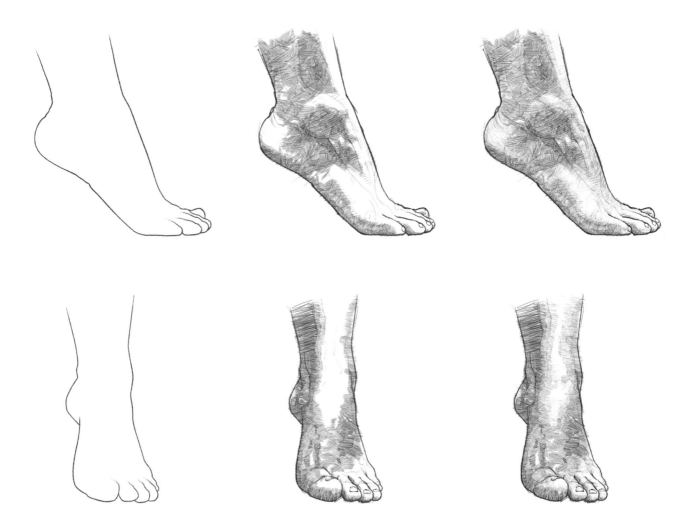

*When drawing feet, start by drawing a light outline of a foot first. Start with the outside view. Study where the light hits the foot and where shadows are created. Slowly, add more definition to your drawings. Repeat these steps each time you draw from a different angle.*

## EXERCISE 2: THE LAST

**MATERIALS:** Pencil; paper; last.

This exercise will create familiarity with the dimensions of the object considered to be the "heart" of the shoe—the last. As before, draw the last from the side first. You will need to prop the last up in order to get the correct angle of the finished shoe since the last does not have a heel or a sole (when propping up the last, leave about ½ in. space under the front and more under the bottom, depending on heel height). Again, draw the last from all possible directions, starting with the side view and moving to the back, front, top, and so on.

*Draw the last from different angles. Prop it up, preferably at correct heel height. At first, draw just the outline and observe where the shadows fall. Then add more definition to give greater dimension.*

## EXERCISE 3: THE SHOE

**MATERIALS:** Pencil; paper; shoes.

The best way to understand some of the basics of shoe drawing is to sketch shoes from your own closet. Pay close attention to the stitching and to how the laces are crossed, as well as to the textural differences between various materials. One of the most common mistakes made when drawing shoes is to show the buckle pins pointing in the wrong direction (they should point in the opposite direction to the end of the strap, see p. 147). You also need to pay attention to the volume and layers of materials that make up the sole. Soles are often mistakenly drawn as one line when, in fact, the sole has quite a bit of thickness to it. Draw your shoes from various angles, paying special attention to the details of the buckles, laces, heels, and tips of the shoes.

*Practice drawing using your own shoes as models. The more you draw actual shoes, the better you will become. Stand them in different positions and learn to see how they look under different lights. You can also try drawing them in pairs. As with the foot and last, start by drawing the whole shoe outline and then slowly fill in the shadows and definition.*

## DRAWING DETAILS

One of the most common problems when drawing shoes is a lack of understanding of how a shoe is constructed. This is why it is important to make a shoe physically at least once or twice, in order to gain a fuller understanding of the object you are designing. The dimensionality and placement of details, such as stitching, is often not drawn clearly. This is acceptable if the drawing is a creative illustration where mood is a priority and clarity is not. However, when creating something more realistic, such as a line drawing (and especially a technical drawing), the accuracy of drawing should be as close to reality as possible.

The best way to get the dimensions and details correct is simply to practice drawing shoes over and over again from life. The easiest way is to start with a very light pencil outline. This will help you to place the details correctly. When drawing, the simplest and most effective way to add depth and dimensionality to the shoe is by adding shadow. Study existing shoes and note how and where the shadows fall. Just a light touch of shadow will bring your drawing alive. Buckles and heels are perfect areas to add shadow to bring out the shape in the shoes. It is also good to start practicing drawing details, not only from a fully flat side view, but also from a three-quarter view. First draw a slightly turned side view, then proceed to a full three-quarter view. Here we have demonstrated how certain details can be drawn.

### Upper

Carefully study how the pieces of the upper fit together, particularly where the stitching lines show how the shoe is sewn together. There are numerous different ways to sew leather and other materials together. Sometimes the lining is even simply glued to sections of the upper. Stitches can be drawn in different ways, such as short lines, a length of dots, and so on. Stitching on its own can also be used as decoration. Whatever style of drawing you use, try to draw the stitching as straight as possible.

*A simple line with no stitch marks (as in this example across the tip) would indicate a stitched and pulled seam, or a hidden stitch line.*

*The side of the line on which the stitches are drawn shows how the shoe is made. In this example, the shoe pattern is stitched on top of the tip piece and the stitches have been drawn to the right of the line.*

*Always draw stitches where they need to be. Look at your own shoes as a reference.*

*In this example the tip piece is sewn on top of the pattern, so the stitches are drawn to the left of the line.*

Decorative surfaces and larger leather grains are sometimes hard to draw by hand, but there are tricks to produce effective surfaces. One such trick is to take a piece of leather with a strong grain (for example, python or alligator print) and place it under your shoe drawing. You can then rub over the surface of the paper using, say, a colored pencil, so that the pattern of the leather is embossed on your drawing. You can also try this method with netlike materials, or even lace—one of the hardest things to draw.

*Making a crayon rubbing of different types of animal skin can help you see how to draw it.*

*The insole is normally thicker in the heel area than the toe area. Also pay attention to how the upper is sandwiched between the insole and the outsole and platform.*

*Elastic in the back of this sling back is exposed.*

Another important part of the upper to which you need to pay attention is the straps. See how they slot over each other, and especially note how sandal straps are pressed between the outsole and the insole.

Peep-toes are a type of shoe that are commonly drawn incorrectly. The trick here is to make sure that both the insole and the outsole show clearly at the front. This will also make your drawings seem three-dimensional.

Piping is a common feature used in shoes and can be drawn as a simple continuous strip of material, with a visible stitch line or not depending on the design.

*A stitch under the edge of the running line indicates a piping.*

## Sole

The sole is often drawn incorrectly as a single thin line. If you look at the actual sole of a shoe, you will notice that it has quite a bit of volume. So it really should be drawn as a thicker line since the bottom part of the shoe is usually composed of the outsole and the insole. Often shoes also have a midsole—or "rand"—a thinner strip of decorative material between the upper and the sole. You therefore need to draw it with a thicker line or shape. Also notice how the outsole of a woman's shoe usually thins down to a line that goes under the heel, or wraps down to the inside of the heel, often called the Louis Heel.

The drawing of the sole should also indicate the material from which it is made. A crêpe sole, for example, would be more uneven than a normal leather sole, and so should be drawn with an uneven line. The bottom of the sole can also have numerous design features that will show on both a side view and a three-quarter view, such as a special grip design.

Women's shoes often have a platform that raises the front part of the shoe. The platform can be covered by the same material as the upper. A drawing showing a separate platform needs a line to demonstrate this dividing "edge," otherwise it could look as though the material should cover the platform.

*A line separating the top and the platform indicates that the shoes have a normal platform added on.*

*Shoes always have a sole and it always needs to be drawn. Pay attention to where the sole ends; in this example it continues down the inside of the heel.*

*When there is no line between the platform and the top of the shoes, it indicates that the shoe is over-lasted, ie., the upper is pulled over the platform.*

*In this example, the sole thins in the under part of the heel.*

## Heel

Heels come in many different shapes and sizes. Some come as a premanufactured sole–heel unit that has no visible line separating the sole from the heel. This is apparent in plastic-bottomed platforms. Most heels, however, are a separate unit that is screwed to the outsole of the shoe and needs to be drawn as such. On heels it is essential to draw the heel cap. All heels have a heel cap to prevent wear and tear of the heel itself.

A shoe has an elegant curve that dips down from under the heel to the ball of the foot. The line from the inside of the heel should follow this curve toward the middle of the shoe.

Heels are usually made from plastic and covered either with real leather or with man-made materials manufactured to resemble stacked leather. Heels can also be made from wood or materials made to resemble wood. A wedge can also be made in many different shapes and from many different materials. A wedge needs to be drawn with an outsole if the heel is formed as a separate part; it would need to have a heel cap drawn as well. Wedges are often made from cork, which can be drawn using a random placement of shapes and lines.

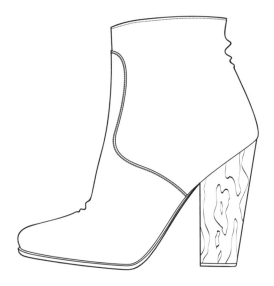

*Surfaces can be made to look like material by simple, drawn-on effects, as seen here with lines that imitate wood grain.*

*Horizontal lines in the heel signify the look of a stacked heel. Heels nowadays are not really stacked but covered with a material that gives the impression of stacked leather.*

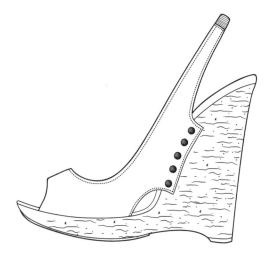

*Cork is commonly used for wedges. The surface effect can easily be imitated by using various markings and lines.*

## Hardware and ornaments

Hardware and ornaments, such as buckles, laces, and other closures, when drawn in detail with additional shadow will add depth to a drawing. Once again the study of real footwear can help you to draw them more accurately.

Observe carefully how the straps go in and out of the buckles, and make sure that the pin of the buckle points in the right direction—opposite to the direction of the strap.

Lacing is sometimes difficult to draw. It is important to draw clearly the parts of the lace that go across and in and out of eyelets. It is usually not necessary to draw the inside area of the lacing between the upper and the tongue because this can create a messy result. The laces and the material of the laces should add texture to the drawing. Remember, even laces have volume and should not be drawn as just single lines going in and out of the eyelets.

*Sneaker lace effect can be achieved by adding crisscross texture to the lace. As seen here it does not have to be done all the way.*

*One of the most common mistakes is when the pin in the buckle is drawn pointing the wrong way. The pin should always point in the opposite direction to the end of the strap.*

*A standard shoelace with added shadow brings a little depth to the drawing.*

*By adding shadow you will make components such as a buckle feel and look more real. Practice with your drawing and observe where the shadows fall.*

*You can alter a shoe's identity by adding details that reference the look of the shoes. Here skate hook eyelets, thicker woven laces, padded ankle, and outsole tread all signify the mountain boot inspiration for these shoes.*

*A ribbon should have volume, and the tiny lines in the bow with clipped tips enforce the idea that it is a ribbon lace.*

*Zippers can be placed in shoes in numerous different ways. Here the zipper is covered with the pattern that overlaps the back part of the boot.*

*By adding a fine line to the edge of a lace you will give an impression of a leather cord that is also often used as a lace, especially in boat shoes.*

*Side zippers are most commonly exposed and stitched on with a double stitch.*

Zippers are one of the most difficult things to draw. How a zipper is placed, and whether it is concealed by a leather flap or not, needs to be indicated clearly. Zippers in general can simply be drawn using three vertical lines with crisscrossing lines. When accurately drawn, it is the pull tab that makes the zipper visually believable. The triangular shape of the zipper slide is quite standard, but the pull tab can be extended and decorated with leather or any other material that is strong enough to be pulled on constantly.

*In this version the zipper is mostly covered by both patterns, front and back.*

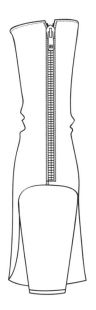

Elastic gussets and elasticized areas, especially around the top of the leg of a boot, are easy to draw, and can be best achieved by drawing thin vertical lines. It is again important to be consistent with the spacing and the uniform thickness of the lines to give a good impression of an elastic panel. Most commonly, elastic is used in side panels of Chelsea boots, at the top of a boot leg, or in a sling-back heel strap.

*Zippers can be hard to draw but paying attention to the pull will make the zippers look more real. Also, a straight line with steady cross lines will give an impression of a real zipper.*

*Elastic can be drawn by simply using vertical lines to give an impression of the lines of an elastic band.*

*It is good sometimes to indicate whether the shoe has a zipper on the inside, especially if a technical drawing is done and the inside is not included.*

*The elastic in the strap of this sling back is mostly covered in leather.*

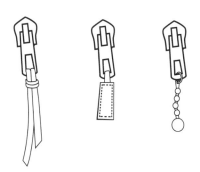

*Adding zipper pull decorations can bring that extra element of reality to your drawings.*

## EXERCISE 4: CONTINUOUS LINE DRAWING

**MATERIALS:** 8½ x 11 in. paper; 0.5 mm micron black ink pen; a shoe.

Take an 8½ x 11 in. sheet and fill the page with a single shoe drawing (use one of your own shoes as a model). The key thing is not to lift your pen from the surface of the paper. Starting with the silhouette, use one continuous line to do this (feel free to go over the same line more than once, if necessary, in order to keep pen on paper). This exercise is great for curbing the temptation to use an eraser, and learning to navigate around the page.

*The best way to get practice in fluid drawing and looser handwriting is to practice with actual shoes. Try to see how far you can go with this by adding details and shadowing as well.*

It is important to experiment with different techniques and materials in order to find alternative ways to express yourself.

### Watercolors

Watercolor is a quick and easy way to establish a "base" color upon which to build your design. Begin by using a shoe that is easy to color, such as a brown one (black is the most difficult because of the need to show form through shading, but this can be mastered with some practice). Draw the shoe very lightly with a mechanical pencil. Do not apply pressure, but use very light strokes for the general dimensions.

Mix a very light watercolor with water. If your brushstrokes get too watery, use tissue paper to absorb the excess. Do not try to fill the drawing completely with color. Allow the base color to dry. Add shadows either using a darker shade of color on top of the base, or using a lighter-colored brush marker (which is water-soluble and blends nicely with watercolor, especially if the surface is still moist). Continue to build on this base as much as you like.

*Annejkh Carson's pencil drawing shows how you can get very soft and textural drawings. Sometimes it is good to use pencil as a light base for your rendering. The next stage would be to slowly add color to it.*

*Watercolor is quite difficult to get used to, but after some practice it is fun to use and the results can be amazing, as in this Annejkh Carson design.*

*Annejkh Carson's drawing using markers shows how the same shoe can have a different feeling depending on which rendering technique is used.*

## Markers

Markers can be very effective even when mixed with more traditional rendering methods—especially for sneaker design. They are widely used in the sports design industry. Using markers can be difficult at first, but after some practice good effects can be achieved.

*With markers you can get very strong and sporty drawings that are perfect for denim-driven streetwear and footwear. In these drawings by Michael Brown you can feel his love of shoe design.*

*This drawing by Georgina Taylor shows how markers can also have a very sensitive and feminine finish.*

CAD, or Computer Aided Design, is used within the industry at many levels. In CAD programs, such as Shoemaster or Lectra, work is done on a last that has already been scanned into a computer, so that the design is done directly on to the last. The patterns can then be sent directly to the client or the factory. Learning CAD takes time, and professional training is required. CAD can also be used creatively to design heels and outsoles or solve more complicated designs.

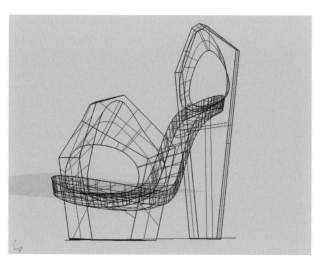

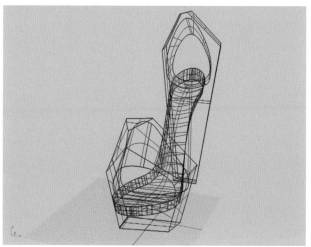

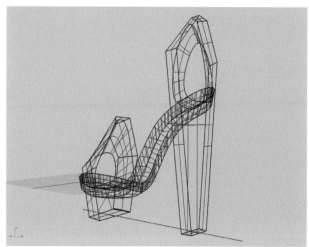

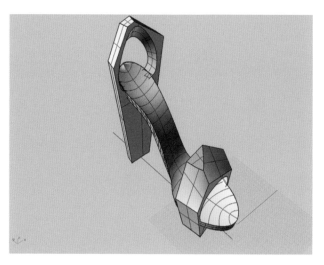

*CAD (Computer Aided Design) programs are often, though not here in Chau Har Lee's designs, used in sports and performance wear. It is a useful skill to have if looking to work in larger companies that use this technology.*

# TECHNICAL DRAWINGS AND LINE DRAWINGS

Technical drawings and line drawings are essentially the same thing: both are clear drawings of your shoes, but technical drawings would have additional specific information, such as detailed measurements, to explain how the shoes are to be made. Line drawings are drawn simply to illustrate the design of your shoe (without measurements) and can be presented alongside artistic illustrations or in a collection lineup presentation.

The drawings are usually made in one of two ways: by hand or using Adobe Illustrator. Freehand drawings are acceptable on an individual designer level, but most larger brands require Illustrator artwork. Nevertheless, a freehand drawing can be almost as good as an Illustrator file. In both cases it is important not to use any artistic license or stylization. This type of drawing is used to show the technical aspect of your drawings and the functionality of your work, so the drawing should be as clear as possible.

You need to show all aspects of the shoe. If only the outside-facing side of the shoe is drawn it is assumed that the inside is the same. The best way to show a technical drawing is from both sides and from the top (outside-facing, inside-facing, and overhead views of a shoe), especially if there are details that are not perfectly symmetrical on both sides. Do not forget that you need to think in three dimensions.

Technical drawings are the communication between the designer and the manufacturer. Hence it is vital that the information is as complete as possible and the drawings are at the right scale, which is a good reason for using the actual last as a base for your drawings. In technical line drawings there should not be any stylistic license; draw the lines as they would look on a real shoe. In general, the drawings will be sent via e-mail to the manufacturer to produce a sample. The basic rule is to keep the drawings simple, clear, and labeled with essential information. By this stage it is likely that you, either on your own or with the manufacturer, will have already sourced the last, heel, and the rest of the components, so this is just to tell the manufacturer how to put it all together. It is also a good idea to send a colored version of the line drawing to give a more realistic view of how you expect the final shoe to look.

## Heather Blake

| | |
|---|---|
| **START DATE** | June 1, 2009 |
| **COMPLETION DATE** | July 31, 2009 |
| **SEASON** | Spring/Summer 2010 |
| **COLLECTION** | "Serpentine" |
| **NAME** | "ARNO" |
| **NUMBER** | SE.SS10.09 |
| **VERSION** | 1 CORAL |
| | |
| **LAST** | 2074492 Formificio Romagnolo |
| **HEEL+height** | Wooden wedge, 5¾ in. |
| **HEEL COVER** | natural wood, wax finish |
| **SOLE** | Natural sueded finish |
| **THREAD** | weight 60, color tone on tone |
| **BRAND** | Embossed on sock, copper foil |
| **FASTENINGS** | Elastic covered in leather |

| | MATERIAL | SUPPLIER | COLOR | CODE |
|---|---|---|---|---|
| **UPPER** | kid | Conceria Gaiera | coral | 4490 |
| **LINING** | kid | Conceria Guerino | natural | C109 |
| **SOCK LINING** | kid | Conceria Gaiera | coral | 4490 |
| **INSOLE BINDING** | kid | Conceria Gaiera | coral | 4490 |

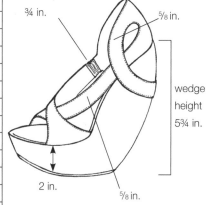

¾ in.  ⅝ in.

wedge height 5¾ in.

2 in.  ⅝ in.

VERSION 1
Coral kid

In general, the drawings will be sent via e-mail to the manufacturer to produce a sample. The basic rule is to keep the drawings simple, clear, and labeled with essential information. Here you see Heather Blake's spec sheet and the final sample.

## EXERCISE 1: FREEHAND TECHNICAL DRAWING

**MATERIALS:** 8½ x 11 in. paper; 0.5 mm mechanical pencil; 0.5 mm micron black ink pen; 1 mm black marker; eraser.

### STEP 1

On 8½ x 11 in. paper, use the pencil to draw a sketch of the shoe with all the details included.

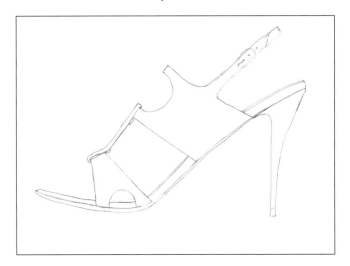

### STEP 2

Rub out most of the pencil line, so that only a faint image is left. Retrace the details with the ink pen.

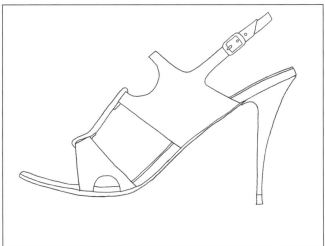

### STEP 3

Then trace the outer line of the drawing with the thicker marker.

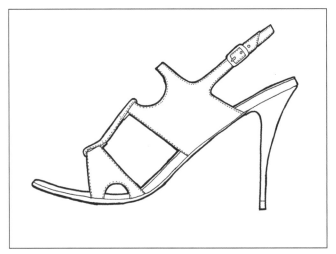

### STEP 4

Scan and shrink the image to the size needed, or copy the 8½ x 11 in. drawing to 30 percent of its original size.

Making your line drawing smaller, either with a scanner or with software, straightens lines but also emphasizes any problems with perspective, which would then need to be corrected.

The information you should add to a technical drawing greatly depends on your audience. If you use the line drawings to clarify your illustrations, then measurements and other technical details are not needed. If you send the line drawings to a manufacturer then technical information should be included. If the last and the sole are already sourced you might want to add the model numbers of those. If this is your first communication with the maker who will source the materials for you then it is advisable to do a full design pack with detailed information, which would include the technical drawings, illustrations, and color and material references.

## COMPUTER SOFTWARE

Computer software enables you to add textures and surfaces to your drawings. A hand-drawn starting point, such as a simple line drawing, with computer enhancements will give the best results. A fully computer-rendered illustration, especially if not done very well, can be cold and spiritless. The computer is, after all, producing the illustration based on your programming. You therefore need to become proficient with the computer software. To experiment you can start by using a simple color-drop technique, and later move on to leather and other materials. Most computers come with some kind of image-editing program, but Adobe Photoshop is the most popular with professionals. You will find virtually endless ways of working with Photoshop—but to get you started, the following pages show some very basic and quick ways to add color, texture, and shading to your product.

*In this sneaker design by Michael Mack the hand-drawn starting point has been enhanced on the computer by adding textural interest and shading.*

## EXERCISE 2: HOW TO RENDER A LINE DRAWING

**MATERIALS:** Computer with Adobe Photoshop; a completed line drawing.

**STEP 1**

Open Photoshop and import your scanned drawing (choose the Black and White/Line Drawing option) by choosing either **File** > **Import** and selecting the name of your scanner or **File** > **Open**.

**STEP 2**

After your image appears in Photoshop, click on **Image** > **Mode** > **Grayscale**.

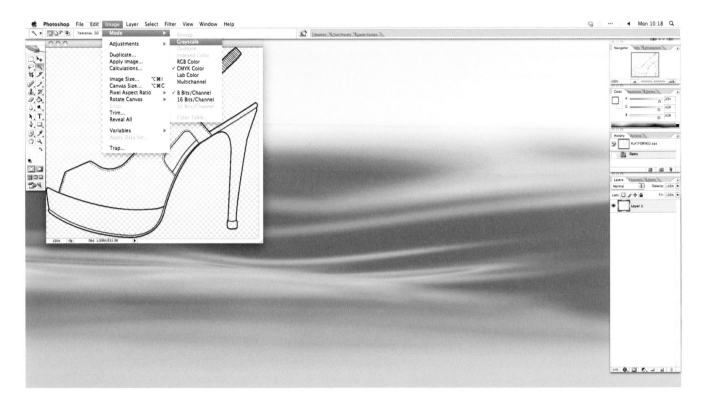

## STEP 3

Then click on **Image** > **Mode** > **RGB Color**.

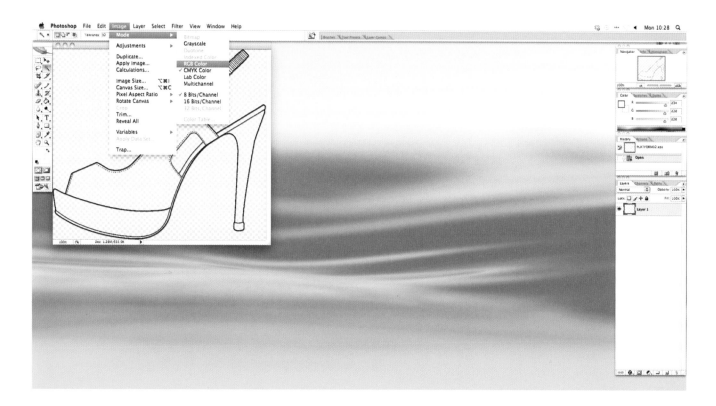

## STEP 4

Select a color you want to use from the Color Picker menu
(right click).

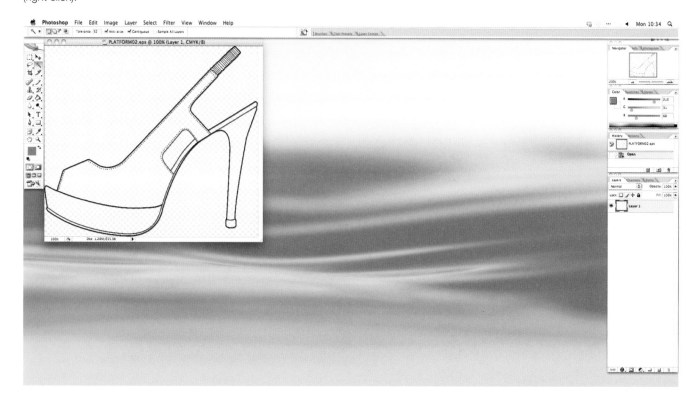

## STEP 5

Click on Paint Bucket tool.

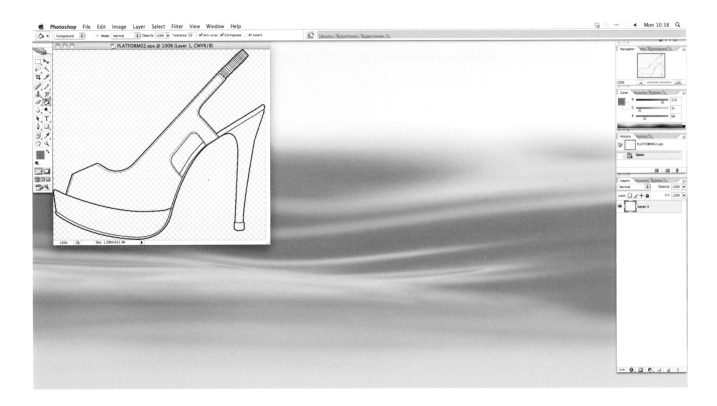

## STEP 6

Click on the area you want to color and the color will fill the space.

## STEP 7

Use other tools to add depth to the drawing: for example, you could use the Darken option of the Pen tool to add shadow (this option is 7 percent opacity with a gray base).

## EXERCISE 3: HOW TO ADD MATERIAL SURFACES TO A LINE DRAWING

**MATERIALS**: Computer with Photoshop; a completed line drawing.

### STEP 1
Open Photoshop. Import your scanned drawing to Photoshop (choose the Black and White/Line Drawing option) by choosing either **File** > **Import** and selecting the name of your scanner or **File** > **Open**.

### STEP 2
After your image appears in Photoshop, click on **Image** > **Mode** > **Grayscale**.

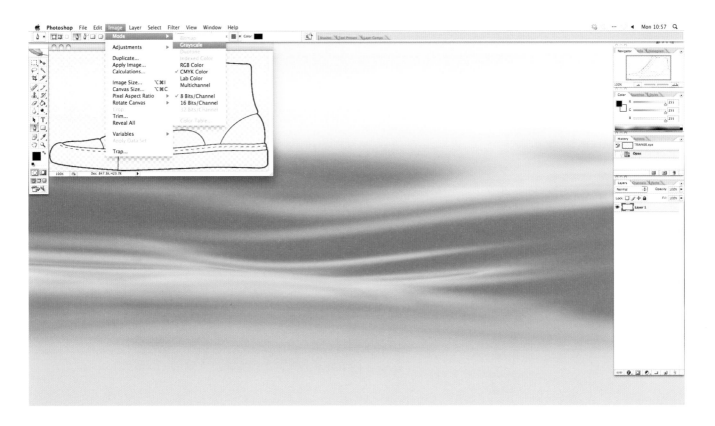

## STEP 3

Then click on **Image** > **Mode** > **RGB Color**.

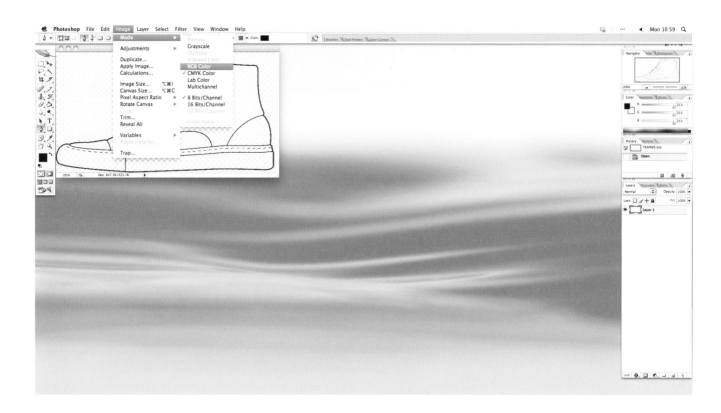

## STEP 4

Scan and import a swatch material (in color).

## STEP 5

Select the area of the swatch (using the Marquee tool) in order to add the swatch to the Pattern library. After selecting it, click on **Edit** > **Define Pattern**. After naming it, the pattern is now saved in the library.

## STEP 6

Open your line drawing in Photoshop. Use the Magic Wand to select the area into which you would like to drop the material.

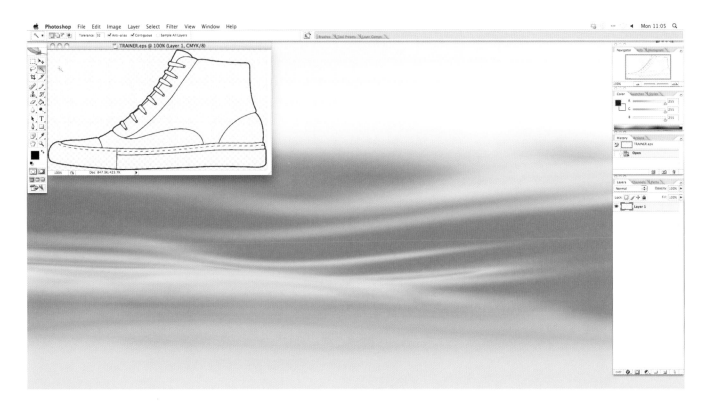

## STEP 7

Go to **Layers** > **New Fill Layer** > **Pattern**.

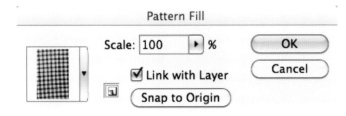

## STEP 8

Click **OK** to make the pattern options come up. Then you can play with materials, scale, etc.

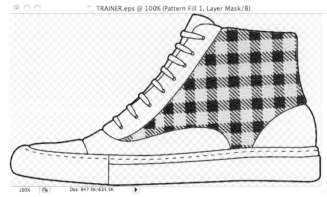

## STEP 9

Repeat this for all the sections in the line drawing of a shoe. Select **Layer** > **Flatten** to flatten the image before continuing to work with textures and colors.

# MIXED MEDIA

There are other, less traditional ways to communicate your design, including collage and mixed media. Collage, three-dimensional ideas, and even film and installations can be effective means of expressing your creativity. Sometimes an installation can send a stronger message than a traditional presentation. Ideas can be delivered in digital format as well. More and more students opt for computerized storytelling, combining hand-drawn images with photographs and even animation.

When mixing hand-drawing with computer-rendering there is really no limit to your creativity. When presenting ideas, designs, or concepts on paper you are immediately limited by the flat two-dimensional surface; when creating something in three dimensions a new emotional element is added. With film and moving image other senses can be included in the experience. Sound is not usually included in traditional presentations (let alone smell or taste), but with the advent of digital media sound can enhance (but also detract from) a presentation. The main focus of designing a collection is the collection itself and, more specifically, the shoes. Do not let the presentation, if produced in mixed media, overshadow and thus maybe ruin the collection—or worse, overshadow your design. Again, there is no "right" way to do this. Follow your instincts.

*Julia Lundsten's FINSK label uses other media to deliver her design message, as shown in this short film.*

Rui Leonardes mixes powerful, inspirational images with his designs and material swatches, creating an instantly engaging visual that tells the story.

# THE DESIGN PACK

A design pack is a complete professional delivery of your design concept. A classic design package would include mood, materials and color, illustrations, and flats or technical drawings. This is not necessarily the only way to present a design, but these are the recommended presentation ingredients. The package is presented either to your academic audience (with the focus on creativity) or to a manufacturer (with the focus on technical aspects and not so much on the mood).

*Start the design pack with a mood board to create a stage for your collection, such as this one by Michala Allen. This way you will lead the viewer to see the collection the way you intend it to be viewed.*

*Not everything is possible in every period.....*

*A range plan with all the technical details leaves no questions unanswered, and provides a clear overview of the footwear in Michala Allen's collection.*

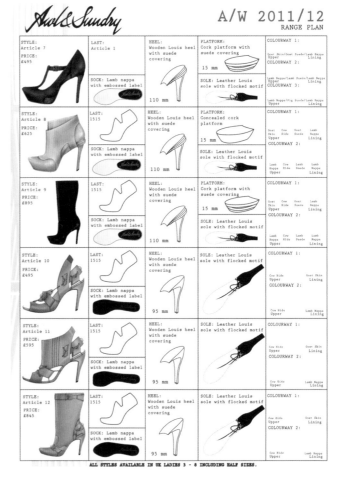

**Aval & Sundry** — A/W 2011/12 RANGE PLAN

| STYLE | LAST | HEEL | PLATFORM | COLOURWAY |
|---|---|---|---|---|
| Article 1 — PRICE: £295 | 1641 — SOCK: Lamb nappa with embossed label | Knock on wooden heel with suede covering — 25 mm | Cork platform with suede covering — 8 mm / SOLE: Knock on Leather sole with flocked motif | 1: Goat Skin/Goat Suede/Lamb Nappa Upper/Lining; 2: Lamb Nappa/Lamb Suede/Lamb Nappa Upper/Lining; 3: Lamb Nappa/Pig Suede/Lamb Nappa Upper/Lining |
| Article 2 — PRICE: £365 | 1515 — SOCK: Lamb nappa with embossed label | Wooden Louis heel with suede covering — 120 mm | Concealed cork platform — 25 mm / SOLE: Leather Louis sole with flocked motif | 1: Goat Skin/Goat Suede/Lamb Nappa Upper/Lining; 2: Lamb Nappa/Lamb Suede/Lamb Nappa Upper/Lining; 3: Lamb Nappa/Pig Suede/Lamb Nappa Upper/Lining |
| Article 3 — PRICE: £845 | 1515 — SOCK: Lamb nappa with embossed label | Wooden Louis heel with suede covering — 120 mm | Concealed cork platform — 25 mm / SOLE: Leather Louis sole with flocked motif | 1: Goat Skin/Cow Hide/Goat Suede/Lamb Lining Upper; 2: ...; 3: ... |
| Article 4 — PRICE: £495 | 1515 — SOCK: Lamb nappa with embossed label | Wooden Louis heel with suede covering — 110 mm | Concealed cork platform — 15 mm / SOLE: Leather Louis sole with flocked motif | 1: Goat Skin/Goat Suede/Lamb Nappa Upper/Lining; 2: ...; 3: ... |
| Article 5 — PRICE: £625 | 1515 — SOCK: Lamb nappa with embossed label | Wooden Louis heel with suede covering — 110 mm | Cork platform with suede covering — 15 mm / SOLE: Leather Louis sole with flocked motif | 1: Goat Skin/Lamb Suede/Lamb Nappa Upper/Lining; 2: ...; 3: ... |
| Article 6 — PRICE: £395 | 1515 — SOCK: Lamb nappa with embossed label | Wooden Louis heel with suede covering — 110 mm | Cork platform with suede covering — 15 mm / SOLE: Leather Louis sole with flocked motif | 1: Goat Skin/Goat Suede/Lamb Nappa Upper/Lining; 2: ... |

ALL STYLES AVAILABLE IN UK LADIES 3 - 8 INCLUDING HALF SIZES.

**Aval & Sundry** — A/W 2011/12 RANGE PLAN

| STYLE | LAST | HEEL | PLATFORM | COLOURWAY |
|---|---|---|---|---|
| Article 7 — PRICE: £495 | Article 1 — SOCK: Lamb nappa with embossed label | Wooden Louis heel with suede covering — 110 mm | Cork platform with suede covering — 15 mm / SOLE: Leather Louis sole with flocked motif | 1: Goat Skin/Goat Suede/Lamb Nappa Upper/Lining; 2: Lamb Nappa/Lamb Suede/Lamb Nappa Upper/Lining; 3: Lamb Nappa/Pig Suede/Lamb Nappa Upper/Lining |
| Article 8 — PRICE: £625 | 1515 — SOCK: Lamb nappa with embossed label | Wooden Louis heel with suede covering — 110 mm | Concealed cork platform — 15 mm / SOLE: Leather Louis sole with flocked motif | 1: Goat/Cow/Goat/Lamb Upper/Lining; 2: Lamb/Cow/Lamb/Lamb Upper/Lining |
| Article 9 — PRICE: £895 | 1515 — SOCK: Lamb nappa with embossed label | Wooden Louis heel with suede covering — 110 mm | Cork platform with suede covering — 15 mm / SOLE: Leather Louis sole with flocked motif | 1: Goat/Cow/Goat/Lamb Upper/Lining; 2: Lamb/Cow/Lamb/Lamb Upper/Lining |
| Article 10 — PRICE: £495 | 1515 — SOCK: Lamb nappa with embossed label | Wooden Louis heel with suede covering — 95 mm | SOLE: Leather Louis sole with flocked motif | 1: Cow Hide Upper/Goat Skin Lining; 2: Cow Hide Upper/Lamb Nappa Lining |
| Article 11 — PRICE: £595 | 1515 — SOCK: Lamb nappa with embossed label | Wooden Louis heel with suede covering — 95 mm | SOLE: Leather Louis sole with flocked motif | 1: Cow Hide Upper/Goat Skin Lining; 2: Cow Hide Upper/Lamb Nappa Lining |
| Article 12 — PRICE: £845 | 1515 — SOCK: Lamb nappa with embossed label | Wooden Louis heel with suede covering — 95 mm | SOLE: Leather Louis sole with flocked motif | 1: Cow Hide Upper/Goat Skin Lining; 2: Cow Hide Upper/Lamb Nappa Lining |

ALL STYLES AVAILABLE IN UK LADIES 3 - 8 INCLUDING HALF SIZES.

*Michala Allen's illustrations, accompanied by technical details, will help the manufacturing process and provide a good visual representation of the end result.*

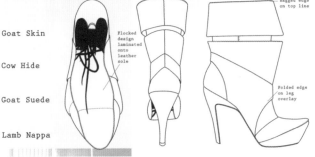

Goat Skin

Cow Hide

Goat Suede

Lamb Nappa

## MOOD

This needs to be demonstrated, as discussed earlier, to explain to your audience the theme or the starting point of your collection. Usually presented in the form of a mood board (see pp. 70–71), it can also be a film or a three-dimensional object that relates to your mood. It is perfectly acceptable to show something like this alongside your traditional mood board.

## MATERIALS AND COLOR

The color references, with samples of the physical materials, give a good indication of the finished collection. Materials, such as leathers and textiles, can be simply composed in relation to an inspirational color image, or they can be shown more creatively in collage or a similar format. It is helpful also to have relevant Pantone color swatches (see pp. 76–81 for how to compose a color and materials board).

## ILLUSTRATIONS

The illustrations should evoke your mood. They should be inspirational and full of emotion. If you do not want to express your collection illustratively you need to find another way of doing so. A well-illustrated presentation can sell your collection.

## LINE DRAWINGS

Line drawings can be displayed on one page to present a good clear overall view of the collection. The drawings do not need to have technical details or multiple views, unless you want to send the information to a manufacturer or maker.

Always take a completed sketchbook to your presentation, whether it is an academic presentation, a presentation to a manufacturer, or even a job interview, just in case you need to show your research and design development.

*Michala Allen's final shoe demonstrates the end result of her extensive research project, design development, illustration, and technical drawings.*

# PORTFOLIO

A portfolio is about your work. It is about the way you think and design. It should clearly represent you as a designer and creative thinker. It also should show your thought process in different projects, and your approach to design. A well-presented collection of work is essential in order to get ahead in this highly competitive field. A poor presentation in cheap plastic covers is not acceptable. Whoever is looking at your work will notice elements such as price tags left on materials or an inconsistent layout.

Your design can be creative, but your portfolio should avoid an overly theatrical style of presentation that could overwhelm and detract from the work you are showing. As we have seen earlier (p. 136), most of the top European fashion houses state that a "hand-drawn portfolio is essential." It is also important to include something in your portfolio that you can leave behind, such as a card and résumé. The three basic areas to consider when preparing your portfolio are size, content, and order.

## SIZE

The standard portfolio size is 11 x 17 in., portrait. Owing to the horizontal nature of footwear it is sometimes easier to think of footwear in a landscape format, but a nice arrangement in a portrait format is recommended. Portrait is also easier to read with one hand standing up, if you need to present your work to someone quickly and without a table.

## CONTENT

The content should show who you are as a designer. The focus should be footwear, but you can also show your strengths in other creative fields. The most important issue is to show your drawing style. The portfolio should show freehand sketch styles, as well as clear line drawings. If you have computer drawing skills you can show these, too. The more skills you demonstrate, the better. The layout of pages is also very important.

Always use a consistent system of layout between your pages or spreads. You can add consistency by using the same font and title placement across the portfolio. This will make it clear and easy to follow. Always give your design work center stage.

*Keep all images in your portfolio in the same viewing direction; this will make them easier to handle and understand, as seen in this Michala Allen portfolio.*

## ORDER

One common question often asked about a portfolio concerns the order in which you should show your work. The answer is that it really depends on your audience. If you show your portfolio for college entrance exams it is necessary to show progression, but when looking for a design job placing the best work at the front will give the best impression of your design ability. Some think that it is good to show the progression and development of the designer, but it is generally the first few pages and seconds that will form the opinion of the viewer. If you are showing the portfolio to a fashion house it is important to focus on creativity, but also demonstrate drawing styles and ideas expressed in sketch format. If you are showing the portfolio to a more mainstream company then a focus on well-drawn, and perhaps more commercial, styles is important. It is good to show both in the very early stages, to demonstrate not only your creative ability but also to show that you can take this creativity to a commercial level. You should have a clear separation between different projects to avoid them blending into one another.

In summary:

- **The simpler, the better.**
- **Do not add an overwhelming design to the cover of the portfolio. This can make the viewer form an instant opinion of you before even examining the contents.**
- **Take references such as manufacturers' stickers off the cover or the spine of the portfolio.**
- **Remove all price tags.**
- **Cater the content to your viewer.**
- **Present your best work first if to a prospective employer.**
- **Use the same layout system throughout.**
- **Clearly separate projects with a title page or separator.**
- **Nonbound portfolios can work well, since the work can be spread around a table. Conversely, a bound portfolio can be viewed if you have to make an instant presentation standing up. Choose your portfolio according to the situation in which you are most likely to find yourself.**

*Digital portfolios, like this one by Chris Van Middendorp, are more and more common and easy to send electronically. The online recruitment professionals and colleges often display students' work in an electronic portfolio format.*

# AFTER GRADUATION

Every spring and summer the fashion and footwear job market is flooded with new design graduates. The question is how to get noticed in this highly competitive marketplace. Positions are few and far between, while the candidates are many.

## GETTING A FOOT IN THE DOOR

The good news is that there may be many more job opportunities than it at first appears, if you research further and spread your net wider. One way to stay a step ahead of the pack is to start early—begin contacting potential employers a few months before your graduation. This would mean getting in touch with designers, brands, suppliers, design houses, and recruitment agencies directly as well as early. You can send them a card, an e-mail, a notice of the up-coming shows with a sample design, or anything to make you stand out in their memory. Later, when they receive a formal invitation from your college they are more likely to recall your name. Most commonly, recruitment agencies (and larger design studios that design for multiple brands) will either visit your final show or arrange to view your work privately.

Another good way to research the job market well before graduating is to sign up for free e-mail notices of job postings (from numerous web-based organizations). This in itself will provide valuable information—who is hiring, how often, what salaries are like, and so on. You should also start networking and making connections as soon as possible with others in the industry. Most countries have trade bodies that deal specifically with footwear professionals, which can provide helpful information. Blogs and social sites also cater to footwear professionals by providing a platform where you can meet like-minded people; trade shows are also a great place to meet other designers. So being proactive is the key to making a good start after graduation.

Nonetheless, having work experience is the most valuable marketing tool when applying for a job. Recruitment agencies, equally, tend to prefer students who have some work experience, as this makes it easier for them to market you. Most agencies plan on visiting the graduate shows anyway—another reason to treat your final collection and presentation with complete professionalism. While presenting your final college collection, always be prepared by having to hand your portfolio, business cards, and résumé—you never know who will walk into your area to discuss your work. Another important thing to remember is that agencies are paid by the companies that are searching for designers, and not by you: stay away from recruiters that want any payment from you in order to find you a job.

## THE INTERVIEW

Once you have secured an invitation to your first interview, there are some things to take into consideration. Remember to research your potential employer, and know what the brand or the design agency is all about. How many do they employ, what other businesses do they conduct? This will serve to give you more confidence at the same time as signaling to a potential employer that you are serious about the position. Tell yourself that you are in the driver's seat, and don't go into an interview with an air of desperation, willing to accept any job immediately. Sometimes the role is just not right for you. First and foremost you have to work out whether you can gain experience from the possible role. Is there opportunity for growth, and is it something you can imagine yourself doing for the next few years?

During the interview the focal point and main representation of your talent will be your portfolio. As discussed in the presentation section, it should be clear, professional, and geared toward your interviewer. Make sure you have a concise, well-written, and, above all, correctly spelled résumé. A footwear design résumé does not really differ much from any other résumé. It is principally a factual information reference, so once again stick to the point. There are a few cultural differences among some nations as to how a CV should look and what it should include, so make sure that you research those nuances when applying in other countries. Fortunately, there are numerous free downloadable samples online. It can be helpful to bring along a few samples of shoes that you have either made or had produced, in order to show that you can make the connection between 2-D and 3-D; however, most of your potential future employer's interest will be in your drawing and design skills.

During your interview the standard rules apply: pay attention; look frequently into the eyes of the interviewer; if you do not know the answer to something do not make it up. Prepare for the commonly asked questions, including "What are your goals?," "What can you bring to the company?," and "What are your strengths and weaknesses?" Most interviewers make up their mind about a person almost immediately, so the best advice really is to be natural and true to yourself.

### Dos and don'ts when creating a résumé:

- At the top include name, complete address, telephone number, and e-mail address. In some cultures, date of birth and marital status are recommended. Keep your résumé all in the same font, but you can play with sizes, boldness, and italics to create an impact.
- Do not include social network profile links, or strange-sounding, complicated, or excessively long e-mail addresses.
- The first paragraph should create a strong professional profile. It should include your skills and a general overview of what you are all about professionally.
- Education: List your most recent degree up-front (even if you have a few weeks to officially complete it), followed by one line for each additional diploma and/or certificate program. If you have little or no work history then add more detail to the items above, as well as high-school information, in order to beef up your education section. Make sure to include any specialist programs completed.
- Experience: Include a complete work history, starting with the most recent position. If the position is ongoing, describe it in the present tense. If the position has ended, keep it in the past tense. State your most recent role first, and work backward in time. Do not lie or exaggerate, but do try to sell yourself by including action verbs within positive phrases that describe your role. If you have worked in a luxury brand showroom answering phones and fetching coffee, make sure the description sounds professional ("Luxury showroom liaison handling customer service, etc."). You can always discuss the specifics at the interview.
- Skills in languages: If you mention that you are fluent in a language, it means fluency in reading, writing, and speaking—all of which you may be asked to do in a new job. In this case, be prepared for a face-to-face or telephone language test. If you are unsure or uncomfortable working in another language all the time, it is better to clarify this in your résumé by mentioning it as, for example, a "basic working knowledge of Italian" or "able to read and write some business French."
- Competitions and exhibitions: If you have participated in any competitions or exhibitions or shows include these as well. Do not mention what your competition placement results were unless you were the winner.
- Activities and interests: This is optional and can tell more about you as a person. However, note that this information may be open to misinterpretation, and so is often better left out of your résumé (and perhaps discussed at the interview instead).
- References: "Available on request" is always recommended. This way you can alert your referees to be ready for someone to contact them.

**Key things to consider at an interview:**

- Be on time. If any problem occurs let them know immediately. Never keep interviewers waiting.
- Be pleasant and professional immediately.
- Always shake hands, looking the interviewer in the eye. Do not interrupt when spoken to. Have your portfolio in top condition.
- Personal appearance: No matter how casual the label or office might be, always dress professionally. This is also culturally interesting, since many still recommend a suit and tie. This may not be the best choice for a performance sportswear company interview, so use your own personal judgment, while keeping well-groomed and wearing clean clothing.
- Also pay attention to personal hygiene, and have well-groomed hands. After making shoes by hand for months, we know what nails, ink, and burning glue can do to your fingers!
- Invest in good and beautiful footwear. When interviewing for a job in the shoe world this will be the first thing that will be noticed. You are, after all, a shoe designer.
- Confidence: The confidence and excitement boost during an interview should be completely natural. Do not pretend to be someone that you are not.
- If the interview is taking place in a more informal environment, such as a restaurant, do not drink alcohol or smoke, even if offered. Subconsciously this will send the wrong message.
- When describing your work do it with pride. It is your work, after all. Never say something such as "this one wasn't a good project." Always focus on the good points and sell yourself.

## ON THE JOB

Once you have been hired, you will most likely be asked to perform junior tasks at first. Additional and greater responsibilities will be added after you have learned the ropes. One of the most time-consuming jobs in any design house is to produce the complete design package—initial ideas, through specific detailed drawings with colored options, to final technical drawings with measurements and material details. Some brands need to produce thousands of drawings before choosing the few that will comprise the final selection. One of your first tasks may therefore be to take designers' sketch ideas and turn them into computerized drawings. On-screen they can then be cleaned up and refined into realistic line drawings, which will then be rendered with shadows and textures. The technical details are added when the sample goes to production. Undertaking such work may not be very exciting, but drawing and getting these packages together is good experience. Of course, different companies work in different ways and some might give you more creative opportunities, but the first few months are usually spent learning the basics. The usual career path is often a few years as junior designer, followed by a senior design position. After extensive experience, a design director job would be the next logical step.

A senior designer would most likely be overseeing the work of junior designers, and would have more decision-making power as to which designs to develop into final prototypes. The position often requires travel to factories to approve the final prototypes before they can appear in the marketplace. At this level you would also develop color stories, and research materials by visiting raw material shows (often with the junior designers). Some larger footwear companies have color and materials specialists, but more often such roles would fall to the senior designer.

The general head of the department is the design director. He or she might oversee a single design department (such as menswear, womenswear, or childrenswear), including providing direction for the junior and senior designers. The director would have the final say on the outcome of the collections, and would work closely with marketing and sales teams to monitor sales performance. This may include dealing with many departments in order to ensure that communication between the designers and the rest of the company works smoothly. A design director's job is basically to ensure that the designs stay within the brand identity but are at the same time exciting enough for the consumer. A global vision, creativity, the ability to multitask and think strategically, combined with strong leadership skills and years of experience, are often required.

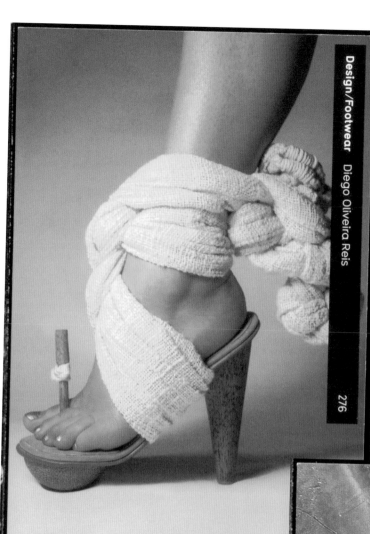

*The final show in your college is your opportunity to network and meet potential employers. At London College of Fashion the graduates not only present their work but also hand out postcards containing essential contact information.*

MADE TO LAST

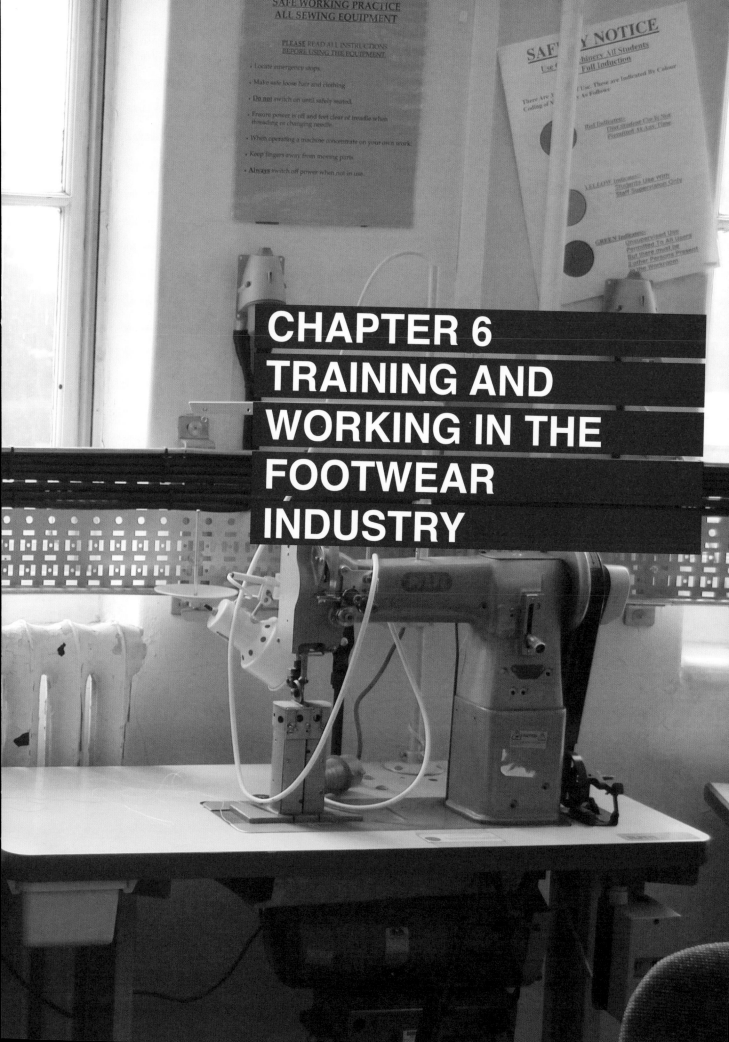

# CHAPTER 6
# TRAINING AND
# WORKING IN THE
# FOOTWEAR
# INDUSTRY

**Footwear design is one of the most exciting and important careers in fashion. In this book we have looked at how to put together a well-designed and attractively presented footwear collection. In doing so we have discussed research—how to compile it and how to develop the material, how to design a collection, how to create flat drawings, and ultimately how to present your work. Of course you cannot become a footwear designer just by reading a textbook. As with any profession, footwear design requires in-depth education, training, and experience.**

To become a successful footwear designer you need, first and foremost, to love shoes. If you can see yourself spending your life completely immersed in the world of shoes, then you have made the right career choice. A passion for fashion and the fashion world is almost equally important. The design world can be great fun and rewarding, but the road to a comfortable level (in terms of both financial status and job security) can be a long and hard one. This is why it is important, as with any job, to do what you love the most (see case studies).

Typical skills required include:

- An ability to communicate designs based on a brief
- An understanding of the manufacturing process
- An understanding of materials
- Creative awareness
- Commercial awareness
- Computer literacy in basic design software
- An understanding of the customer
- An ability to communicate design in a relatively small surface area (shoes)
- An ability to work under pressure
- An understanding of the client
- An understanding of the technical aspects of shoemaking

# TRAINING

One of the most common questions is: "What is the best way to break into a footwear career?" Luckily there are many different ways to approach the study of shoe design. Numerous design schools offer short programs of study in footwear design and shoemaking. It is advisable to try one of these "taster programs" for ideas on which direction to take, and they are usually evening, weekend, or vacation programs. They are generally broken down into design and technical (or making) programs. The design program would be similar to the format of this book—to help a student put together a small portfolio of work, with an inspirational starting point and final illustrated collection. Technical programs usually cover the basic construction of a shoe, such as a ballerina or court shoe. Eventually you might specialize in one of many different options, from sandal-making to proper boot-making. It is a good idea to take programs in both design and making to see if the shoe-design world is something of interest.

A full degree in footwear can take up to three or four years and requires much more of a commitment. Generally the first year of a degree would cover basic drawing techniques, including the basics of sketching, and rendering techniques such as watercolors and markers. Most colleges will also start with sewing techniques, where students will need to create a folder or a book demonstrating technical aspects of making. This would include sewing methods, how to attach hardware to uppers, and numerous other ways to treat shoe parts. Pattern-making might also be included, starting from simple patterns, such as a court shoe or derby, to more complicated examples, such as a boot. Students may be making shoes and working on college-set design briefs in addition to projects that are often set by local footwear companies. The first couple of years of the program will generally involve design tutorials combined with creating collections with handmade end results. The last year is often dedicated to designing a final collection that will showcase your design identity. Preparations for the real world, such as portfolios and résumés, will also usually be part of the final year of study.

In addition to undergraduate degrees, some design schools offer graduate degrees. In graduate programs students are usually expected to excel in the concept of footwear design, and will be expected to create a collection demonstrating their individual style and displaying their own personal design "handwriting."

*Grace Zhong is a good example of how learning all the steps from the very beginning can add advantages to your prototyping skills.*

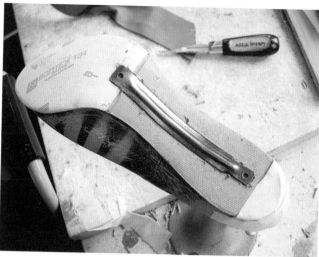

*Grace Zhong slots the shank into the insole board. The shank is an essential part of high-heeled shoes that you never actually see.*

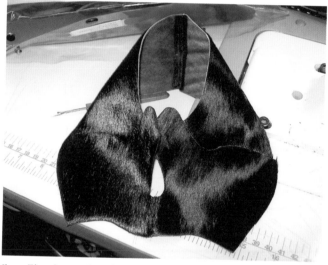

*Grace Zhong's upper is ready to be lasted over the last shape and the insole.*

*It is vital to know the production aspects from the very beginning in order to become a better shoe designer. In Grace Zhong's Black Beauty-inspired shoe the form, the materials, and the feel of the shoe follow her theme closely.*

# FOOTWEAR CAREERS

Throughout the book we have discussed the various options available to you in a career in footwear design. Selected case studies include careers as a designer, maker, trend forecaster, or teacher, among other options. The main career options are summarized here.

## FOOTWEAR DESIGNER FOR A LABEL OR A DESIGN STUDIO

The most popular option, and possibly the easiest option for those new to the field, is to become a footwear designer for a brand or a design office. Working under a design director, the job would initially involve administrative duties with some drawing. This is why it is important to be able to do illustrations by hand and by computer; the company you work for might want you to work in one way or the other. Companies will generally train junior designers so that they are able to increase their responsibilities. This might involve international travel to trade shows and factories.

Most brand and label design jobs involve fulfilling the company-set briefs and design guidelines and you would need to understand these and be able to design collections that fit the parameters. You would also need to have a good understanding of materials, color, and trend information.

Most brands have in-house designers, but many also outsource their jobs to design studios. A studio might be designing for several brands, and is often subdivided internally so that each designer focuses on certain labels. The design studios work closely with the brand. This sometimes includes the sourcing of production, and dealing with the complete delivery—working from design concept to final product.

## FREELANCE DESIGNER

Typically a freelance designer will be contracted by either a label or a design house to create a collection for them. You will need to be able to design within the brief of the company, and thoroughly understand the needs of the client. Depending on the company, it will probably be sufficient to present your work using the design pack as explained in this book. You will need to explain each stage of your design development, and present a final illustrated design with clear flats. Often freelance designers are asked to communicate with the factory in order to follow the process of creating a final prototype.

However, to become a successful independent designer years of experience are required and it is not, therefore, for the newly graduated. Networking and keeping numerous up-to-date design contacts are essential to make it in the freelance market. Most of the time freelance positions appear via agencies or previous work contacts. Knowledge of trends and the ability to work independently (but also working within a given brief) are important skills to have for this type of design work. The obvious downside of being a freelance designer is the lack of job security, but on the positive side the pay is substantially higher for contract work.

## SHOEMAKER

A career in shoemaking involves working in a niche market and requires a multitude of very specialized skills. Shoemaking is a craft-based career, and the ability to work well with your hands is essential. A standard footwear education combined with an apprenticeship is the normal route to becoming a shoemaker. Generally, bespoke (made-to-order) shoemaking is for menswear, but there are numerous makers who focus on women's shoes as well. The best path is to take a technical course, as mentioned earlier, to see if that is something that feels natural. Makers usually have their own facilities, which involves investing in tools and some machinery. As well as having their own private clients, they often work on a freelance basis for other bespoke shoemakers.

*To become a good shoemaker requires years of experience and knowledge of all the right techniques and tools to become a master of the trade. Sebastian Tarek uses a great variety of tools and instruments to make his shoes.*

# CASE STUDY: RACHEL JONES

Rachel Jones is a footwear designer and trend consultant based in London, UK. After graduating from Cordwainers College in 2001 she started working as a footwear editor at WGSN, a leading trend forecasting service. Along with her trend work, she worked as a freelance footwear designer before launching her own brand, Rae Jones, in 2008.

**Q How/where do you start with the collection design?**

**A** I am constantly collecting shapes and ideas in my head ready for the upcoming seasons, and so I often have an idea of the types of silhouettes I would like to include. My signature style of "wearable but interesting" keeps the look of the collection fitting for the brand, and of course as the only designer my handwriting is quite distinctive and usually fairly apparent!

**Q When you design a collection do you sometimes/always/never have a theme?**

**A** I generally always have a theme, and as the collection is fairly small I find it very useful for bonding the collection together into a cohesive whole, be it through color, surface texture, or detail.

**Q How do you research your collection (is there a researched story, materials research, etc.)?**

**A** I tend to collect imagery for inspiration of color and surface texture and have an idea of what sort of thing I'd like to do before I start looking at actual raw materials. Then a visit to the leather fair Linea Pelle in Bologna at the start of the season really seals the inspiration into place. It gives me the chance to uncover interesting new leathers and get much closer to where I see the collection going and how it will look.

**Q How do you gather inspirational ideas? Book? Mood board? Mood or ideas wall?**

**A** I have an ongoing selection of folders for each season. As I come across images through all the work I do, I add them in, and then edit just before I start to design or browse through for general inspiration. Should there be anything specific I want to research, I consult the Internet or art and design books for a wider view.

**Q Do you draw the initial ideas in a sketchbook?**

**A** Yes, I draw miniature sketches of ideas and plan out the actual silhouettes and lasts so that I don't waste time just drawing shoes that aren't right or don't fit.

**Q Do you use computer-aided drawing or only draw by hand?**

**A** I draw by hand and then scan the drawings, spec-ing up the designs by computer.

**Q When drawing by hand what materials do you prefer (pens, pencils, watercolors, paper types, etc.)? If drawing by computer, which program do you use?**

**A** I draw in pencil, nearly always a mechanical pencil! And then draw over with a fine liner pen in (very specific here!) 0.5 size for the main lines, 0.3 for stitching, and maybe 0.8 for thicker lines. Then I often outline the external edges (it just looks better!) in a thicker pen before scanning. I use Adobe Photoshop for spec-ing up. I can use Illustrator but just prefer to draw by hand—I like to be old-fashioned, I suppose.

**Q What is the most important part of your design cycle? Theme? Design? Sampling? Production?**

**A** I think design is the most important part: it's easy to miss details out and it's the detail that draws someone to the shoe on the shelf. I think experience teaches you to consider the greater form, how it will look, and what could be added earlier rather than amending at sample stage.

**Q What is the most pleasurable part of the design cycle?**

**A** Starting off, getting leathers, and getting inspired. The world is your oyster and there's almost a sense of trepidation at what could happen and what you could create!

**Q What advice can you give to a budding footwear designer?**

**A** Try not to limit yourself too much with thoughts of commerciality but let your ideas flow and then rework till you're happy with them. Never compromise!

*Rachel Jones's brand Rae Jones combines the English countryside with London's East End to produce a comfortable yet unique look.*

## YOUR OWN LABEL

For many, having a shoe label is the ultimate dream. Having your own footwear label requires extensive knowledge on many levels. The best path to take is to work for a brand and get as much experience as possible, then do a business plan. The more you know of how the "real world" works the less likely you are to make mistakes with your own label: errors mean loss of revenue. Have professionals help with the plan and set realistic goals and follow the plan closely.

Some of the things to consider when running your own label are: design, raw material sourcing, sample making, costing, wholesale, production, quality control, deliveries, customer service, publicity, trade shows, graphics, billing, website maintenance, and the day-to-day running of a business. You might not do all of these tasks yourself, and would have to identify those that you would be able to undertake and those where you might need to employ someone else or outsource the task—an undertaking that involves good communication and management skills. These are just some of the issues you would need to deal with. Some designers consider launching a brand right after graduation, or even without formal footwear studies. The best advice is: don't! Running your own business is hard and requires a multitude of skills. Having said that, if you do have the right personality, funding, determination, experience, and a strong design identity, having your own label and business can be very rewarding.

The competition is tough and hundreds of talented design graduates flood the market every year. There are, however, thousands of footwear brands and labels in the world that are always looking to give opportunities to good footwear designers. Make it a priority to get some work experience during (or in between) your studies. Volunteer a few days a month to help out a designer or a design office to get that valuable experience for your graduate résumé. Several bigger brands also offer formal internship programs. You can inquire within your college, or try to contact companies directly. Another good way to add value to your studies and résumé is to enter international design competitions. Winners usually get a monetary award but also, more importantly, international exposure and opportunities. As with any design career, determination is the key.

There are other opportunities in sportswear, production, and teaching that could also be of interest. The best path, however, is to obtain an educational basis for all these professions. As long as humans continue to walk, there will be a demand for footwear design talent.

*Trade shows offer a great opportunity to network with other footwear professionals, as seen here in a stand at Germany's GDS trade show.*

*Many countries have initiatives to help new businesses to get started. The Topshop-sponsored British Fashion Council New Generation Awards (NEWGEN) has helped designers to launch their labels since 1993.*

# SEASONS AND TRADE SHOWS

Traditionally footwear follows the same two (compound) fashion seasons as apparel—Fall/Winter and Spring/Summer. Although a few companies also produce cruise, holiday, and special collections, footwear trade shows are based on the standard system of two fashion seasons. Collection design usually begins at least one year before the product appears in stores—the process from sample production to wholesaling and final delivery often takes that long. However, design schedules may vary depending on the type and size of company you are working for. Once the collection has been designed, and the sample making organized with the manufacturer, then the product wholesale process can begin. For example, a shoe trade show that takes place in September/October 2011 will have retailers expecting delivery in February/March of 2012. In other words, a fall trade show will be marketing the following year's Spring/Summer season shoes. Therefore, trade shows that take place in February/March 2012 would be showcasing products for Fall/Winter 2012.

Sales can be accomplished via various channels, but since the majority is by agents and distributors in trade shows, these shows have become a top priority for shoe brands. Trade shows serve two main purposes: a) sales and b) press exposure for brands/designers/manufacturers. It is important for any future designer to visit trade shows in order to observe the real-life inner workings of the shoe world. Also, the associated trade events (catwalk shows, lectures, trend seminars, opening receptions, etc.) are important for making business contacts, and offer a great opportunity to network with other areas of the industry. Meeting other professionals is an inevitable part of the process, and shows often have less formal evening events and parties.

Trade shows are generally open only to preregistered industry professionals or members of the press (ie., not the general public), but often do allow students. Nevertheless, you must first contact the show organizers directly—in advance of your visit—for information on preregistration. Also inquire as to which days and times the show is open to students, since student visiting hours may be limited by the trade show organizers. Brands ordinarily welcome students to their stand, as long as they are not too busy with buyers.

Most major fashion capitals host a trade show that includes footwear. But there are only a few trade shows that focus on shoes alone. MICAM, GDS, and WSA are the three main footwear shows that present new collections to the world twice a year:

The Milan-based MICAM emphasizes Italian shoe design, and is the essential show for footwear buyers to attend, due to the high quality of Italian production. This event covers all ranges of footwear, from the most basic to absolute luxury. MICAM also has a special section to showcase non-Italian designer brands; its International Designer Section is reserved for independent designers and small brands. Large international companies are often located in country-specific designated areas such as the Brazilian section or Japanese brands section. MICAM is normally well covered by both the trade and general press, thereby making it a good platform for international publicity.

GDS takes place in Düsseldorf, Germany. It mainly caters to the German market and has a more commercial, business-driven atmosphere. All the major brands show here, in addition to a special separate designer brand area occupied largely by agent or distributor showrooms. GDS also includes the Global Shoes event, where manufacturers from the Far East come and do business in Europe. This section of the show is designed for the international sourcing and volume business. The German market is a key shoe market in Europe, and GDS continues to be an important show for many companies.

WSA is a trade show based in Las Vegas, Nevada, and caters mainly to the North and South American market. European brands are often represented by third parties (or a US-based sales department) in this show, since sales from any country to US retailers requires dealing with more complicated delivery, customs, and tax regulations. WSA has also separated the designer brands from the more commercial brands. The Venetian Hotel hosts the international designers on several floors—designers show their latest creations in their hotel rooms! The WSA show is frequented mainly by North American buyers, but also Central and South Americans.

Cities such as Paris, London, and Milan also offer interesting accessories shows during their "fashion week." One of the most important in the accessories fashion calendar is Première Classe, a show during Paris Women's Fashion Week that features the top creatives of the accessories world. Other fashion weeks, such as at London and Milan, offer exhibitions that are a good mix of apparel and accessories. Menswear seasons also have exhibitions that often have shoes on offer. Pitti Uomo in Florence traditionally opens each buying season with a wide variety of menswear including shoes and accessories. There are also numerous smaller exhibitions that take place during the fashion weeks that offer good opportunities to network within the business.

Trade shows are not limited to high fashion alone. There are trade shows in apparel that cater to denim-driven streetwear, such as Bread and Butter in Berlin. Another large area of wholesale that has some footwear on offer is ISPO in Munich, a show representing the performance sportswear sector. Most of the trade shows mentioned above also have an international edition in various countries.

The best way to understand the intricacies of each market place and trade show is to visit the show in person. Since each show has been designed to cater to a specific type of market with a specific type of product, it makes sense to experience these events first hand.

# CASE STUDY: SUE SAUNDERS

Sue Saunders teaches footwear design in London at Cordwainers College (now part of London College of Fashion) and the Royal College of Art, and a list of her former students reads like a Who's Who of British footwear designers, including Georgina Goodman, Tracey Neuls, Charlotte Delall, and Cleo Barbour.

Saunders began her career in the Swinging Sixties, when jazz and Motown were the order of the day, Honey the style magazine of choice, and designers such as Mary Quant the style icons for young women. She was particularly interested in the independent shoe designs of Moya Bowler—one of the first female footwear designers with her own label. Saunders completed her footwear design degree at Leicester College of Art and Technology in 1968 (now DeMontfort University). After graduation she worked as a footwear designer for more than 20 years. In 1992 she decided to teach one day a week, and slowly moved her career from the design side to the academic side. In 1996 Saunders helped to form the first footwear MA program at the Royal College of Art, which has been running successfully ever since. In 2007 she was made a fellow of the Higher Education Academy, and in 2009 a Freeman of the Worshipful Company of Cordwainers.

### Q What is the significance of education?
**A** Education creates opportunity. It develops knowledge and skills, it creates self-confidence, it gives people credibility in our society, it gives people choice, it often creates an outlet for people's dreams and passions, it gives people an outlet for their energy (something to do that is positive and not destructive), and a sense of belonging to a "tribe."

### Q What is your view on the digitization of work? Does hand-drawing still matter?
**A** Hand-drawing is a key skill for any designer. The direct interaction between the designer and the page is something that can't easily be replaced. The designer will draw the exact form and line that he/she requires without influence from any other interaction. There are still many companies—a significant number at the highest end of the market—that rely purely on hand-drawing.

However, every aspiring designer needs to be able to use computer applications that relate to their specialism. These are valuable for creating clean, clear technical drawings, rendering, adding texture, and creating professionally finished presentation work.

### Q What is the most important thing for a footwear student to learn?
**A** The most important thing is to understand the difference between the last and the finished shoe. The multiple layers that go into making a shoe create a very different final shape from the shape of the last. This needs to be understood fully for a designer to be able to design their lasts to create the final shape required.

Other than that—communication skills to ensure that a sample room will produce a sample that exactly matches the designer's vision. In this global industry a designer cannot always personally oversee their sample production and so needs the correct communication tools to achieve what they want. Hence the need for hand-drawing, clear technical drawings, specification sheets, and a precise administrative system that both parties understand thoroughly.

### Q What would you suggest to a graduating student?

A It goes without saying that a stunning portfolio of work, a strong résumé, and good personal presentation are vital. It is also important to have some work experience. Many students do this during their program of study. Equally they are taken more seriously by the specialist employment agencies. Any student who doesn't have experience should just grab the first opportunity that comes along related to the area they want to work in—whether it's an internship or a low-level job in a design team. It will give them the experience they need to fully understand the whole picture.

It's not impossible for graduates without experience to find good positions, but generally it will only be the most talented and socially skilled that achieve this.

### Q What is the best part of your job?

A Students come into college full of raw enthusiasm. To see them mature and develop as they acquire knowledge and skills is wonderful—it's a joy to be a part of this process. Every year there is a surprise—something that no one has ever created before; it never ceases to amaze me. I enjoy sharing their successes, supporting them through difficult times, and following their careers as they become respected, serious professionals.

*Sue Saunders tutors students in all aspects of shoe design, from concept to realization and even sewing techniques, as seen here.*

# GLOSSARY

**arch** on the foot, the high, curved part of the sole, located between the ball and the heel; on the shoe, a raised area of the insole for padding and support of the arch of the foot.

**backpart** back section of the last.

**back strap** piece of material covering the back seam of the upper.

**ball** the padded area of the foot below the toes.

**bespoke** custom-made, usually by hand.

**binding** decorative or reinforcing trim on an upper or insole.

**box calf** calfskin treated with chromium salts, with a pattern of square or creaselike markings on the grain.

**chrome tanning** the process of tanning with chromium salts, producing a leather that stands up well to industrial production; 80 percent of leather is chrome tanned because it's cheaper and quicker than vegetable tanning.

**color and materials board(s)** boards showing respectively the color and materials direction based on your research; ideally two separate boards but they can be combined.

**cone** the instep part of the last.

**counter** part of upper or lining material that sits in the back part of the shoe.

**counter point** the point where the top line of the heel counter touches the back line of the shoe.

**EVA (ethylene vinyl acetate)** a man-made substance used to make soles.

**facing** front upper pattern piece above the vamp, often where eyelets and lacing is placed.

**fast fashion** a relatively recent market-driven phenomenon in which stores stock quickly changing collections imitating the latest catwalk designs, at a low price point and with a high turnover.

**feather edge** the edge that lies between the last bottom and the top of the last.

**flat** technical or line drawing.

**forepart** the front section of the last.

**heel cap** small plastic tip on the bottom of a woman's shoe-heel, designed to be easily replaced after wear and tear.

**heel counter** a piece of semirigid material (sometimes leather or thermoplastic) that helps in maintaining the shape of the heel cup area and in holding the heel of the foot in place.

**heel height** the measured last heel height.

**heel pitch** the angle of the seat of the last where it meets the heel.

**hinge** the part on the last where the front and the back are mechanically connected.

**insole** the part of the shoe that the foot rests on; often cushioned, it provides structure and shape to the bottom of the shoe.

**insole board** part of the insole, consisting of cellulose board or a composite material, and attached to the shank.

**instep** the inner arched area of the foot between the toes and the heel; or the top front part of a shoe.

**joint** the widest part of the last in the forepart where the foot flexes; on the foot, the joints between the phalanges and the metatarsals where the foot flexes.

**last** metal, wood, or plastic form used to create the internal volume of a shoe.

**lining** material such as pigskin, calfskin, kidskin, or textile on the inside of the shoe to keep the internal parts of the upper in place.

**mood board** board on which is mounted a selection of images to sum up and evoke the results of your research for a collection; to be used as a tool in the development of that collection or when presenting your collection.

**nanotechnology** technology that builds devices by manipulating single atoms and molecules.

**outsole** the bottom part of the shoe that touches the ground, made from various materials including leather, rubber, and polyurethane.

**overlasted** when the upper is pulled over the front platform.

**overmeasure** the space between the tip of the wearer's toes and the end of the shoe, generally $\frac{1}{2}$–$\frac{3}{4}$ in.

**pattern** an actual-size, two-dimensional representation of a last's three-dimensional surface.

**pitch** same as heel pitch.

**quarters** the side panels of the shoe.

**rand** a strip of decorative material between the upper and the sole.

**seat** where the weight rests on the back part of the insole within the shoe.

**shank** on the insole, a supporting bridge between the heel and the ball of the foot; usually a steel strip but sometimes nylon, wood, or even leather.

**skiving** the cutting away of the edge of an upper piece or sole to make it thinner or more pliable.

**sock lining** on the shoe, the surface (leather or fabric) with which the bottom of the foot comes into contact; it covers either the footbed or the insole.

**sole** generally refers to the part below the upper; the bottom of the shoe.

**tanning** the process of making leather from the skins of animals to prevent decomposition.

**technical drawing** line drawing with additional specific information, for example regarding how the shoe is to be made, or measurements.

**thimble** a hole for the lasting pin to go when the last is taken out of the shoe.

**toe box** on the shoe, a piece of semirigid thermoplastic material (sometimes leather) heat-molded to the shape of the toe area, helping to maintain the shape and height of the front end.

**toe cap** pattern piece on the toe of the shoe.

**toe spring** the space between the bottom of the toe of the shoe and the ground.

**tongue** generally found on lace-up shoes, a strip that runs up the top-center of the shoe and sits on the top part of the foot, protecting the foot and preventing the laces from rubbing.

**topline point** generally ¼ in. above the counter point, where the top line of the upper touches the back of the foot.

**topline tape** prevents the stretching of the topline of the shoe's upper while being lasted, and during wear.

**TPU (thermoplastic polyurethane)** plastic material often used in shoe soles.

**upper** on the shoe, everything above the sole; made up of pattern pieces that are sewn together.

**vamp** the forepart of the upper.

**vamp point** a reference point in pattern cutting and upper construction on a last.

**vegetable tanning** the process of tanning using vegetable extracts (tannins), producing a flexible leather that ages well.

**waist** the arch and instep of the foot (or the last).

**welt** a strip of material joining the upper to the sole.

# USEFUL INFORMATION

## BOOKS

Albers, Josef, *Interaction of Color,* Yale University Press, 1963

Choklat, Aki and Rachel Jones, *Shoe Design,* DAAB Publishing, 2009

Cox, Caroline, *Vintage Shoes,* Carlton Books Ltd, 2008

DeMello, Margo, *Feet and Footwear: A Cultural Encyclopedia,* Greenwood, 2009

English, Bonnie, *A Cultural History of Fashion in the 20th Century*, Berg, 2007

Ferragamo, Salvatore. *Shoemaker of Dreams,* Sillabe, 1985 (first edition 1957 by George G. Harrap)

Grewd, Francis and Margrethe de Neergaard, *Shoes and Pattens*, The Boydell Press, 2006

Huey, Sue and Rebecca Proctor, *New Shoes: Contemporary Footwear Design,* Laurence King Publishing, 2007

Kalman, Tibor, *(un)Fashion*, HNA Books, 2005

Levine, Beth and Jonathan Walford: *The Seductive Shoe: Four Centuries of Fashion Footwear*, Thames & Hudson, 2007

Mackenzie, Althea, *Shoes and Slippers*, The National Trust, 2004

McQuaid, M., *Extreme Textiles: Designing for High Performance*, Thames & Hudson, 2005

O'Keeffe, Linda, *Shoes*, Workman Publishing, 1997

Peacock, John, *Shoes: The Complete Sourcebook*, Thames & Hudson, 2005

Pedersen, Stephanie, *Shoes: The Grace, the Glamour and the Glory…*, David & Charles, 2005

Quinn, Bradley, *The Boot*, Laurence King Publishing, 2010

Riello, Giorgio and Peter McNeil, *Shoes: A History from Sandals to Sneakers*, Berg Publishers Ltd, 2006

Seivewright, Simon, *Research and Design,* AVA Academia, 2007

Thomas, Dana, *Deluxe: How Luxury Lost Its Lustre*, The Penguin Press, 2007

Trasko, Mary, *Heavenly Soles*, Abbeville Press, 1989

Vass, Lazlo, *Handmade Shoes for Men,* Konemann, 1996

Walford, Jonathan, *Shoes A–Z: Designers, Brands, Manufacturers and Retailers*, Thames & Hudson, 2010

## WEBSITES/E-MAILS

### Designers/Design companies

Aku Bäckström
  akubackstrom@gmail.com
Annejkh Carson
  annie_carson@hotmail.com
Bart Hess
  www.barthess.nl
Benjamin John Hall
  www.benjaminjohnhall.com
Catherine Willems (footwear anthropologist)
  www.catherinewillems.com
Chau Har Lee
  www.chauharlee.com
Chris Van Middendorp
  www.ifd-dhta.blogspot.com/
Diego Oliveira Reis
  www.diegovanassibara.com

Eelko Moorer
  www.eelkomoorer.com/
Erdem
  www.erdem.co.uk
Erik Bjerkesjö
  www.erikbjerkesjo.com
FINSK by Julia Lundsten
  www.finsk.com
Georgina Taylor
  www.georginataylor.com
Giuliana Borzillo
  giulianaborzillo@yahoo.it
Grace Zhong
  gracezhong.is@gmail.com
Heather Blake
  www.heatherblake.co.uk
Helen Furber
  www.helenfurber.com
Hiroshi Yoneda
  www.cordvan.jp
Jin Hong
  jinhongdesigns@gmail.com
John Galliano
  www.johngalliano.com
Jonas Hakaniemi (product design)
  www.jonashakaniemi.com
Kei Kagami
  keikagami@btinternet.com
Laura Schannach
  laura.schannach@gmail.com
Mark Emmett (pattern cutter)
  emmett_mark@hotmail.com
Marloes ten Bhömer
  www.marloestenbhomer.com
Michael Brown
  www.coroflot.com/
  michaelbrown1984
Michael Mack
  Mimack26@gmail.com
Michala Allen
  micki_allen@yahoo.co.uk
Milan Sheen
  milansheen@gmail.com
Minna Parikka
  www.minnaparikka.com
Noritaka Tatehana
  www.noritakatatehana.com
Oat Shoes
  www.oatshoes.com
Paco Gil
  www.pacogil.com
Rachel Jones
  www.raejones.co.uk
Raffaello Scardigli
  raffaelloscardigli@alice.it
Reetta Mällinen
  reta.raven@gmail.com
Rick Owens
  www.rickowens.eu
Rosanne Bergsma
  www.rosannebergsma.nl
Rui Leonardes
  www.ruileonardes.com
Sandra-Noella Schachenmann
  sn.schachenmann@gmx.ch
Stuart Weitzman
  www.stuartweitzman.com

### Footwear production

D'Alessio Galliano (tannery, Italy)
  www.dalessiogalliano.com
Forever Soles
  www.forever.pt
Pantone (color experts)
  www.pantone.com
Russo di Casandrino (tannery, Italy)
  www.russodicasandrino.com
Sebastian Tarek (shoemaker)
  www.sebastiantarek.com
Springline (maker of lasts)
  www.springline.net

### Graphic designers/Photographers

James Frid
  www.jamesfridphotography.t83.net
Charlie Hunter
  www.flux-art.co.uk
Christian Trippe
  www.christiantrippe.com
Petri Tuohimaa
  www.tuohimaa.net

### International Associations/Sales

**UK**
British Footwear Association
  www.britfoot.com
Footwear Friends (charity to help footwear industry)
  www.footwearfriends.org.uk
**US**
American Apparel and Footwear Association
  www.apparelandfootwear.org
**Italy**
  www.anci-calzature.com
**Portugal**
  www.portugalshoes.com
**Spain**
Federation of Spanish Footwear Industries
  www.fice.es

### Museums

**UK**
The British Museum
  www.britishmuseum.org
Museum of London
  www.museumoflondon.org.uk
Northampton Shoe Museum
  www.northampton.gov.uk
Victoria and Albert Museum
  www.vam.ac.uk/
Wellcome Collection (medical history)
  www.wellcomecollection.org
**US**
FIT (Fashion Institute of Technology)
  www.fitnyc.edu
**Belgium**
SONS – Shoes or No Shoes
  www.shoesornoshoes.com

**Canada**
Bata Shoe Museum
  www.batashoemuseum.ca
**Czechoslovakia**
Zlin Shoe Museum
  www.muzeum-zlin.cz
**Finland**
Vapriikki Shoe Museum
  www.tampere.fi/english/vapriikki/exhibitions/shoemuseum.html
**Switzerland**
Bally Shoe Museum
  www.schoenenwerd.ch/de/tourismus/sehensballyschuhe/
**Germany**
German Shoe & Leather Museum
  www.ledermuseum.de
**Japan**
Japan Footwear Museum
  www.fukuyama-kanko.com/english/hyaka/cat_spot017.html
**The Netherlands**
Virtual Shoe Museum (Liza Snook)
  www.virtualshoemuseum.com
**Italy**
Museo Ferragamo
  www.museoferragamo.it
Museo Internazionale della Calzatura 'Pietro Bertolini'
  www.comune.vigevano.pv.it
**Spain**
Museo del Calzado
  www.museocalzado.com

### News/Information

Footwear News
  www.wwd.com/footwear-news
KCTV
  kctv.co.uk
Shoeinfo
  www.shoeinfonet.com

### Trade fairs/Shows

GDS (Germany)
  www.gds-online.com
Linea Pelle (leather fair, Italy)
  www.lineapelle-fair.it
MICAM (Italy)
  www.micamonline.com
Premiere Classe (accessories, Paris)
  www.premiere-classe.com
WSA (USA)
  www.wsashow.com

### Trend forecasters

Li Edelkoort—Trend Union
  www.trendunion.com
Material Preview
  www.materialpreview.com
Nicoline Van Enter—Ytrends
  www.ytrends.com
Niels Holger Wien
  u2n11@web.de
WGSN
  www.wgsn.com

# INDEX

# PICTURE CREDITS

t = top; b = bottom; l = left; r = right; c = center

Where not mentioned, images are © Laurence King Publishing Ltd

4 Chau Har Lee/Photo James Frid; 6 Heather Blake; 8–9 Corbis/© Mark Blinch/Reuters; 10t © The Trustees of the British Museum; 10bl Getty Images/AFP; 10br University of Oregon Museum of Natural and Cultural History/Photo Jack Liu; 11tl, cl & tr © Museum of London; 11bl © Aki Choklat; 11br Aki Choklat/Photo James Frid; 12t Corbis/© Mark Blinch/Reuters; 12cl The Art Archive/Museum of London; 12cr Noritaka Tatehana/www.noritakatatehana.com; 12b Alamy/© Photos 12; 13t Photo Josse, Paris; 13b © Museum of London; 14t The National Library of Finland; 14b Courtesy of Museo Salvatore Ferragamo, Florence; 15t Getty Images/Estate Of Keith Morris/Redferns; 15b Getty Images/Michael Ochs Archives; 16tl & tr Photos provided by Stuart Weitzman; 16b Getty/WireImage; 17tl "A Hunt for High-Tech," Bart Hess; 17tr Julia Lundsten/FINSK/www.finsk.com/Photo James Frid; 17bl Marloes ten Bhömer; 17br Getty/WireImage; 18l & r Andrew Meredith; 19 Oat Shoes; 20 Courtesy Kei Kagami; 21 Eelko Moorer/Ingrid Hora; 22 Liza Snook; 23 © Virtual Shoe Museum/www.virtualshoemuseum.com: Top—Vegas girl by Iris Schieferstein(Hoof)/ Center rows—Heels by Roxanne Jackson/Huge red cap by Bertrand LandrO/Horseshoes by Iris Schieferstein/Paula, Annie, Rohan, Lieve & Irma by Irma Bruggeman/Hatch by Alexander Fielden/Floor by Irma Bruggeman/Dorothy Wizard of Oz by Barbara Zucchi/Sole mates by Samira Boon/Mongolian boot by Roswitha van Rijn/Vegas girl & Horseshoes by Iris Schieferstein/Brutal Billy goat by Karin Janssen/Baby skin boot by Roswitha van Rijn/Rabbit boot by Rachel de Kler/Moulded Moles by Van Eijk & Van der Lubbe/Strapped Goathair & Goathair Boot by Zjef van Bezouw/Hairy by Julia Veres/Pony by Jan Jansen (© collection Dutch Leather and Shoe Museum)/Yes, I do? & How to tell a fairytale without the skin of colours by Renate Volleberg (photo Riesjard Schropp)/Lick my toes, Horsetail Boots & Funfur by Zjef van Bezouw/Hairy and Karen by Lola Pagola/ Bottom row—Woman's black shoes by Svenja Ritter (courtesy Galerie Petra Nostheide-Eÿcke)/Slide by Kobi Levi/Tisshoes by Masashi Kawamura/Stretching cat by Tetsuya Uenobe; 24 Courtesy Catherine Willems/© Paul De Malsche; 25, 26, 27 Courtesy Catherine Willems/© Kristiaan D'Aout; 28–29 Photo James Frid; 30 Aku Bäckström; 31 Getty/Nick Veasey; 32 Alamy/© Nucleus Medical Art, Inc; 33, 34 Reetta Mällinen; 35, 36 Photos James Frid; 37t Reetta Mällinen; 37b Aki Choklat; 38 Heather Blake/Photos James Frid; 39t Reetta Mällinen; 39b Heather Blake/Photo James Frid; 40 Photo James Frid; 41tl Photo James Frid; 41tr Chau Har Lee/Photo James Frid; 41b Aku Bäckström; 42t Photo James Frid; 42b Aku Bäckström; 43t Photo James Frid; 44t Aku Bäckström/Photo James Frid; 44b Aki Choklat/Photo James Frid; 45c Russo Di Casandrino; 45b Aki Choklat/Photo James Frid; 46-49 Aku Bäckström; 50, 51 Sebastian Tarek/Photos James Frid; 52–53 Laura Schannach; 56, 57t Diego Oliveira Reis; 57c Jin Hong; 57b Diego Oliveria Reis; 58t Benjamin John Hall/www.benjaminjohnhall.com; 58bl & br Helen Furber/Photo David Abrahams/Project sponsored by Y-3 Adidas, Naturally Organic Leather, Studio van der Graaf; 59t Jin Hong; 59c Diego Oliveira Reis; 59b Grace Zhong/Photo Robert Zhao; 60t & b Jin Hong; 61t Diego Oliveira Reis/Image courtesy of KCTV www.kctv.co.uk/Photographer Harris Kyprianou, Styling Justine Josephs assisted by Scott Webster & Julia Dakin, Hair Eiki Nakajima, Makeup Madge Foster, Model Lucianna, sculpted body piece Venice Yu Xaio, Shoes Jean-Charles De Castelbajac; 61c & b Diego Oliveira Reis; 62 Wellcome Images/Rama Knight; 63t Corbis/© Mick Tsikas/Reuters/© Jim Lambie; 63b Michala Allen; 64l PYMCA/Mr Hartnett; 64r PYMCA/David B. Mann; 65tl Laura Schannach/photo on left page of sketchbook © ARS, NY, and DACS, London 2011; 65tr Diego Oliveira Reis; 65b Grace Zhong/Photo Robert Zhao; 66t Diego Oliveira Reis/Photo James Frid; 66b Diego Oliveira Reis; 67tr Laura Schannach; 67b Diego Oliveira Reis; 68tl Diego Oliveira Reis; 68tr Laura Schannach; 68b, 69tl & c Diego Oliveira Reis; 69b Chau Har Lee; 71 Michala Allen; 73 Claudio Scalas & Reetta Mällinen; 74–75, 75t, c & b Aki Choklat; 77 Aku Bäckström; 78–79, 79t Diego Oliveira Reis; 79c Chau Har Lee; 80 Chau Har Lee; 81t Interior Design by Torsten Neeland, Duravit Starck 3/Photo by Rudi Schmutz; 83tl & tr Catwalking; 83 cr Jonas Hakaniemi; 83cl & b Kei Kagami; 84 Nicoline Van Enter; 85 Nicoline Van Enter/www.ytrends.com; 86 Niels Holger Wien/Photo Jo Schaller; 88t & b, 89t & b Niels Holger Wien/Speaking Colours, NHW; 90–91 Jin Hong; 92–93 Helen Furber; 93t Helen Furber/Photo David Abrahams/Project sponsored by Y-3

Adidas, Naturally Organic Leather, Studio van der Graaf; 94t & c Aki Choklat; 94bl & br Georgina Taylor; 95 Georgina Taylor; 96tr Diego Oliveira Reis; 96tl & b Aki Choklat; 97tl Photo courtesy of Petri Tuohimaa; 97cl, cr & b Aki Choklat; 98t & b Aki Choklat; 99tl Photo courtesy of Petri Tuohimaa/Sculpture with permission of Parviz Tanavoli: Big Red Heech, 2001, Fiberglass 290 x 190 x 175 cm (114 x 75 x 69 in.). British Museum, London; 99c & b Aki Choklat; 100 Diego Oliveira Reis; 101t Diego Oliveira Reis; 101b Jin Hong; 102 photos James Frid; 103tl & tr Aki Choklat; 103cl Photo James Frid; 103cc, cr & b Aki Choklat; 104t Kei Kagami; 104b Georgina Taylor/Photo James Frid; 105tl Photo James Frid; 105tr & cr & br Aki Choklat; 106l & r, 107 Aki Choklat; 108tr Chau Har Lee; 108c Aki Choklat; 108bl, bc & br Claudio Scalas; 109tl, tr & b Claudio Scalas; 110t, c & b Georgina Taylor/Photos James Frid; 111 Rae Jones/Photos Sandra Waibl; 112l Aki Choklat/Photo James Frid; 112r Stuart Weitzman; 113 Chau Har Lee/Photo James Frid; 114tl & tr Raffaello Scardigli/Photos James Frid; 114c Georgina Taylor/Photo James Frid; 114bl Chau Har Lee/Photo James Frid; 114br Julia Lundsten/FINSK/www.finsk.com/Photo James Frid; 115t Raffaello Scardigli/Photo James Frid; 115bl, cr & br Aki Choklat/Photos James Frid; 116tl Aki Choklat/Photo James Frid; 116tr Rae Jones/Photo Sandra Waibl; 116bl Aki Choklat/Photo James Frid; 116br Julia Lundsten/FINSK/www.finsk.com/Photo James Frid; 117tr Michala Allen/Photo James Frid; 117 all remaining photos James Frid; 118 Giuliana Borzillo/D'Alessio Galliano/Photos James Frid; 119t Benjamin John Hall/www.benjaminjohnhall.com/Photo James Frid; 119c & bl Aku Bäckström/Photos James Frid; 119br Noritaka Tatehana/www.noritakatatehana.com; 120tl, tr, bl & br Helen Furber/Photo David Abrahams/Project sponsored by Y-3 Adidas, Naturally Organic Leather, Studio van der graaf; 121tl, tr, bl & br Chau Har Lee/Photos James Frid; 122 Noritaka Tatehana/www.noritakatatehana.com; 123t Chau Har Lee; 123b Photo James Frid; 124t & b Minna Parikka/Photos Saila Semeri; 125 Minna Parikka/Photo Aleksi Niemelä; 126t & b Rosanne Bergsma/Photos Simone van Rees; 127 Rosanne Bergsma/Photo Pieter Bouma; 128, 129 photos provided by Stuart Weitzman; 130, 131 Paco Gil; 132–133 Erik Bjerkesjö/Photo Ola Bergengren; 134t & 134–135 Milan Sheen; 135 Sandra Noella Schachenmann/Studioquagli, Florence/Personal support: Aki Choklat/Angelo/Meret Aebersold/Polimoda/Kraus Waldemar; 137 photos © LKP by Fredrika Löckholm & Martin Slivka; 138 Aki Choklat; 139tl, tr, bl & br Hiroshi Yoneda; 140, 141 & 142 Charlie Hunter; 143 Reetta Mällinen; 144tr Aki Choklat; 144l, cr & br Reetta Mällinen; 145–149 Reetta Mällinen; 150t Christian Trippe; 150b Aki Choklat; 151 Annejkh Carson; 152tl, tr, cl & cr Michael Brown; 152b Georgina Taylor; 153 Chau Har Lee; 155 Heather Blake; 156 Aki Choklat; 157 Michael Mack; 164 Julia Lundsten/FINSK/www.finsk.com; 165 Rui Leonardes; 166, 167t Michala Allen; 167b Michala Allen/Photo James Frid; 168 Michala Allen; 169 Chris Van Middendorp; 171 Corbis/© Mike Kemp/Rubberbal; 173t Diego Oliveira Reis; 173b Grace Zhong; 174–175 Photo James Frid; 177 Grace Zhong; 179 Sebastian Tarek/Photo James Frid; 180 Rachel Jones/Photo Gustavo Papaleo; 181 Rachel Jones/Photos Sandra Waibl; 182t Aki Choklat; 182b Courtesy British Fashion Council; 184–185 Photo James Frid

# ACKNOWLEDGMENTS

First I would like to thank the Laurence King Publishing team for taking on this project with such enthusiasm: Helen Rochester for commissioning, Anne Townley and Melissa Danny for editing, and Claire Gouldstone for picture research. I would like to give a special thank you to Geordie Diaz for helping me with the manuscript.

A big thank you goes to Mark Emmett and Heather Blake for making sure all the technical terms and aspects are sound. I would also like to thank James Frid for the photography, Aku Bäckström for early research, and Reetta Mällinen for Illustrator work.

Furthermore, thanks to Michala Allen, Javed Afzal, Beatrice Behlen, Rosanne Bergsma, Marloes ten Bhömer, Erik Bjerkesjö, Giuliana Borzillo, Michael Brown, David Capon, Annejkh Carson, Russo Di Casandrino, Caroline Darke, Sergio Faria, Forever Soles, Helen Furber, D'Alessio Galliano, Paco Gil, Darla Jane Gilroy, Jonas Hakaniemi, Benjamin John Hall, Bart Hess, Jin Hong, Charlie Hunter, Rachel Jones, KCTV, Kei Kagami, Lahtiset, Chau Har Lee, Rui Leonardes, Eeva-Liisa Leppänen, Mari Lind, Linda Loppa, Julia Lundsten, Michael Mack, Eelko Moorer, Patrick De Muynck, Merianne Nebo, Melissa Needham, Oat Shoes, Tomoko Oya, Minna Parikka, Diego Oliveira Reis, Sue Saunders, Kaija Savolainen, Claudio Scalas, Sandra-Noella Schachenmann, Laura Schannach, Raffaello Scardigli, Milan Sheen, Sirkka Siiskonen, Liza Snook, Basia Szkutnicka, Sebastian Tarek, Noritaka Tatehana, Georgina Taylor, Christian Trippe, Petri Tuohimaa, Nicoline Van Enter, Chris Van Middendorp, Masaru Watanabe, Stuart Weitzman, Niels Holger Wien, Catherine Willems, Hiroshi Yoneda, and Grace Zhong.

Finally, I would like to acknowledge the significance of my teachers, colleagues, and students for always providing a stimulating environment for learning. This book is dedicated to all past and future students, for the future of footwear is in their hands.